THE PURE PR

To Joy

THE
PURE PRINCIPLE
Quakers and other faiths

Jim Pym

William Sessions Limited
York, England

Cover photograph of a waterfall in Brunei copyright © Paul Devereux.
Cover design by Jim Pym

Printed in 10 on 11 point Plantin Typeface
from Author's Disk
by Sessions of York
The Ebor Press
York YO31 9HS

Contents

Foreword

WRITING THIS BOOK has been fascinating and frustrating. It has been fascinating to explore the experience of working with Friends in the interfaith field, to remember those events in which I was directly involved, and to research some in which I was not. I have acknowledged in the appropriate section the help that I have received from various Friends and friends, without whom the book could not have been written.

It was frustrating, because so much of the Quaker work in this area has been – and is being – done quietly, often without specific reference to Quakerism, though the subtle influence of Quaker beliefs and practices is always there. In particular, there is Friends' assertion that our sacred and secular lives are not separate. With this work, it is often hard to uncover the full facts, and I have had to rely on the written and verbal records of those involved. Because of this, I have only written about those events and practices which have touched on my own spiritual journey, and so there will be whole areas of Quaker work with other faith traditions which are not recorded here.

Many of the memories of events and the conclusions of Friends, will inevitably differ from those that I have experienced. For example, if – as had originally been intended – Margot Tennyson had written this book, I am sure that it would have been very different, even though many of our experiences were shared. This is not to say that either would have been right or wrong. Because our experiences – objective and subjective – vary, the record of them will necessarily be expressed in different ways. Quakerism is, above all, a 'Way of Experience'.

So I make no apology for writing the book as I have done. If there are any inaccuracies or omissions I apologise for them. I could not hope to include all the activities that Friends have been involved in, nor to represent every point of view within the Quaker world, or even within Britain Yearly Meeting. I hope that readers will accept that I have written it as sincerely and openly as I can, even if they disagree with what I have to say. It represents, at this time, an honest expression of my discoveries, experiences and conclusions. I also hope that others – with different experiences and more knowledge – will find the time to write and share what they have discovered, and what they will certainly discover in the future, for this work is on-going.

The new millennium will see new and significant breakthroughs in Quaker work with other faiths. It will be interesting to discover whether the influences of other spiritual practices on Quakers – particularly with regard to meditation – will increase or diminish. I personally feel they will increase. But I hope that Friends will not forget their roots in the life and teaching of Jesus, and will use them as a firm base to explore other traditions. Whatever happens, I pray that this book will encourage discussion, and be helpful to Friends whose lives are touched by the wonderful world of wider spirituality.

Kingham, Oxfordshire
January 2000

The Pure Principle

There is a principle which is pure, placed in the human mind, which in different places and ages has had different names; it is however pure and proceeds from God. It is deep and inward, confined to no Forms of Religion nor excluded from any, where the heart stands in perfect sincerity.

John Woolman.[1]

✡ ☥ ☾ ✳ ☯ ✾ ॐ

What is God? In the universe, law; in the conscience, goodness; in the mind, truth; in nature and art, beauty and order; in the heart, love.

Bradford Smith.[2]

✡ ☥ ☾ ✳ ☯ ✾ ॐ

The aim or purpose of each religion is to cure the pains and unhappiness of the human mind. Here too, it is not a question of which religion is superior as such. The question is, which will better cure a particular person.

H.H. The Dalai Lama.[3]

✡ ☥ ☾ ✳ ☯ ✾ ॐ

What is my religion? My friends, my teachers, my God. And who is my God? He speaks within me; if I mishear, my friends correct me; if I misdo, I look to Jesus Christ. How then am I taught? I hear in the silence, I ponder in solitude, and I try in the noisy crowd to practise it. What do I learn? To put gaiety before prudence, grace before pleasure, service before power. What am I commanded? To seek patience in suffering, humility in success, steadfastness always. What is forbidden me? To reject another's love, to despise another's wisdom, to blaspheme another's God. And to what purpose? To help others, that we may enter the Commonwealth of Heaven together. each to find our Being in the Whole.

Frederick Parker-Rhodes.[4]

Acknowledgements

THERE ARE A NUMBER of people without whom this book could not have been written. The story of interfaith work in the UK, and particularly among Friends, is mostly the story of individuals and their vision. Some of these people I know only through their writings. Others have been friends and teachers – to say nothing of Friends and teachers – and I am grateful to all of them. If I list some and omit others, it is because those listed have had a direct influence on the part of my life that is concerned with interfaith work.

First must come Margot Tennyson, who should have written this book, and who inspired me more than I can say to work in the field of encouraging Friends to look at – and learn from – other faiths. Margot fell ill when she should have been writing, but recovered enough to give shape to her concern that the Millennium, though primarily a Christian festival, should also be celebrated with an interfaith dimension. She suggested the "Millennium Interfaith Celebration of Universal Love", and this caught the imagination of other Friends. With the help of Alec Davison and The Leaveners (Quaker Arts Projects), this was launched at an event at Friends House on the 18th April 1999, and we are all grateful to them for the work that they did in helping this to happen. Unfortunately, Margot once again became very ill some time before the event, and was not able to attend, but I know that she was with us in spirit. She died the following day. The event was a great success, and an account of it – and matters associated with it – appears in Appendix 2.

Alec Davison was also a great help in reading the manuscript, making helpful suggestions, and seeing the book through to final publication. David Goddard, friend and former colleague in the Literature Section of Quaker Home Service, has edited this manuscript, given great support and provided many helpful suggestions. In some ways I have been too close to the subject, and it needed a clear eye, backed by a sound knowledge both of Quaker practice and of the beliefs and practices of many other traditions. David has provided this, and I am most grateful. Harvey Gillman, another former colleague at QHS, was also very helpful with a number of suggestions.

In the general interfaith field there was Sir Francis Younghusband, whose vision led to the founding of the World Congress of Faiths, without which many of us – including myself – would never have become involved in the interfaith scene. Then there was the Rev Jack Austin, Buddhist priest, Anglican chorister and for some time Secretary of the WCF. In an obituary for the journal, *The Shin Buddhist*, I called him "A Bridgebuilder for the Light", and that is what he was to me. He was a good friend and a wise teacher. Tom Gulliver was also deeply involved with the Friends Interfaith Group and the World Congress of Faiths, and was the inspiration behind the Buddhist-Christian Dialogue Group which has met faithfully for more than ten years.

Damaris Parker-Rhodes' Swarthmore Lecture, *Truth, a Path and not a Possession* kept me within the Society of Friends, and gave me one of the first glimpses of the broader canvas that is possible for Quakers. She and Frederick, her husband, gave us friendship, understanding and many insights for which I will always be grateful. Clare Cameron, poet, mystic and 'spiritual mother' to Beryl and I, was editor of H.T. Hamblin's *Science of Thought Review*, but had also edited the Buddhist journal, *The Middle Way*. She helped us reconcile Christian and Buddhist thought through her words and silence. She had a deep understanding of Friends, and was an occasional attender at Chichester Meeting.

Among Friends that I did not know personally, but who influenced me through their writings, are Douglas Steere, whose work on what he called "Mutual Irradiation", and his pamphlet of the same name gave us the key to all the work of the Friends Interfaith Group, and much more besides. Pierre Lacout's miniature classic, *God is Silence*, has spoken to me almost since I first met Friends, and drew me into a realisation that this really is so, and made it easier to find God with all who love stillness, whatever their labels. Bradford Smith's book *Meditation, the Inward Art*, deserves to be better known by Friends, both here in the UK, and in the United States. He was – as far as I know – the first Friend in modern times to write about meditation and worship as a single subject.

There have been spiritual teachers from other traditions whose message was of the Oneness from which all religions spring. Among those who have had the greatest influence on me are Joel Goldsmith, mystic, spiritual healer and author of more than 20 books who has been – and still is – a great inspiration; Sri Ramana Maharshi, the sage of Arunachala, and Sri Nisargadatta Maharaj of Bombay taught me the importance of knowing the Self; while Roshi Furukawa, of the Seimeizan Schweitzer Temple in Japan, who works with people of all faiths, has shown me how the universal Light of the Buddha leads us in the path of Peace and Compassion, in a way that is very close to that of Friends.

My wife, Beryl, as always, has supported me in my writing, given encouragement, and even made me take breaks for tea. We have journeyed the Spiritual Path together, and to her I cannot say enough in gratitude.

Then there was Joy, who had a deep concern that the interfaith work of Friends should be carried forward, and who left funds for a book to be written and published. The book is dedicated to her. Joy lived her life in communication with a Higher Source, which gave her guidance, companionship and deep tranquillity. She had her own high standards which she lived by, and I hope that this writing meets with her approval.

Last, but not least, there are the officers and members of Hampstead Monthly Meeting who have acted as stewards for the funds, and thereby enabled publication.

I would like to specifically express my gratitude to the following for quotations from various works published by them. Full details will be found in the Bibliography:

Paul Devereux for the cover photograph.

Britain Yearly Meeting: *Quaker Faith and Practice*.

Quaker Home Service: *Truth, a Path and Not a Possession* and *The Way Out is the Way In* by Damaris Parker Rhodes; *Friends and Other Faiths* by Margot Tennyson; *God is Silence* by Pierre Lacout; *A Minority of One* by Harvey Gillman; *Images and Silence* by Chris Cook and Brenda Heales.

The Buddhist Society, London: *The Goose is Out* by W J Gabb.

Pendle Hill Publications: *Mutual Irradiation* by Douglas Steere, and Scot Crom's *Quaker Worship and Techniques of Meditation*.

Sessions of York: *Transcending Tradition*; *excerpts from the writings and talks of Marjorie Sykes* compiled and edited by Martha Dart; and her *Marjorie Sykes, Quaker Gandhian*. Also *Pilgrims in Hindu Holy Land* by Geoffrey Waring Maw, edited by Gillian M (Maw) Conacher and Marjorie Sykes.

George Allen and Unwin: *Meditation, the Inward Art* by Bradford Smith

Oxford University Press: *The Upanishads*, trans. Patrick Olivelle; *Journal and Major Essays* of John Woolman.

Riders: *A Manual of Zen Buddhism* by D T Suzuki.

The Ramakrishna Vedanta Centre: *The Gospel of Sri Ramakrishna (Abridged Edition)* by 'M', translated by Swami Nikhilananda.

Friends Historical Society: *The Journal of the FHS*, vol. 55, No 8, the article 'Some Notes on George Fox and Islam' by N I Matar.

The Seekers' Association for quotes from *The Seeker*.

The Quaker Universalist Group for quotes from *The Universalist*; and for *Quakerism as Forerunner*, by John Linton.

Fellowship in Prayer: *Tao, Way of the Ways* by Herrymon Maurer.

Jeanette Bossert, for permission to quote from her unpublished manuscript, *Journey into the Orient*.

Yukio Irie for his translation of Hakuin's *Song of Meditation*, and for *A Zen-Christian Pilgrimage*.

Oneworld Publications for *A Wider Vision – A History of the World Congress of Faiths* by Marcus Braybrooke.

Introduction

THE WORLD TODAY is one in which there are a multitude of beliefs and traditions seeking to co-exist and make their mark. Religion is something that is, on the one hand, ignored by many people, and on the other, a source of conflict which still leads to polarisation of views, often to an extreme degree. There is also a paradox that, in a time of increasing religious fundamentalism, there is also a great fusion of ideas, a willingness to understand the faith of others, and to work together for the greater good of the world in which we all live, and in particular for those who are suffering. This begins at the level of shared spirituality rather than shared religion. A shared spirituality, often based on silence, allows religious understanding to come about in ways that will never happen if we start from the level of language and belief.

This idea of shared spirituality is not new, but it is something that has grown with the increase in communication. As we shall see, Quakers have had some knowledge of other spiritual systems from the earliest times, and as a people who saw themselves as reviving the spirit of earliest Christianity, they were also a part of the shared spirituality of the time of Jesus. Current research is uncovering just how many influences came to make up what we call Christianity. The travellers on the Silk Road who brought ideas from the East; the beauty and wonder of the Jewish tradition; the 'pagan' influences of Greece, Rome and the Celts; and the influences of Zoroastrian dualism all had a part to play in what we call Christianity today.

The middle of the nineteenth century brought new impetus to what has become the 'interfaith movement'. Even Queen Victoria, for some an archetype of conservative morality, was a contributor to this change of thought. In 1858, she issued a proclamation, part of which read:

> Firmly relying ourselves on the truth of Christianity and acknowledging with gratitude the solace of religion, we disclaim alike the right and desire to impose our convictions on any of our subjects. We declare it to be our royal will and pleasure that none be in anywise favoured, none molested or disquieted, by reason of their religion, faith or observances ....[5]

We may, with hindsight, criticise the application of such a desire, but at least the spirit was there.

Towards the end of the nineteenth century, there occurred an event which was unique, and which is felt by many to be the start of the present interfaith movement. This was the World's Parliament of Religions, which was held in Chicago in 1893. A second 'Parliament' was also held there in 1933. In London, there was a "Religions of Empire" conference held in conjunction with the British Empire Exhibition, and one of the conditions was that each speaker should be practitioner of the religion on which they spoke. Also among the speakers was Sir Francis Younghusband, who gave the opening address. Sir Francis was the rare combination – even today – of statesman, adventurer and mystic, and he had many personal spiritual experiences which led him to found the World Congress of Faiths.

The World Congress of Faiths was originally the title of yet another conference, held in 1936. The Congress itself was a grand affair. Among the speakers were Dr Yusuf Ali, translator of the Qur'an; D. T Suzuki, whose writings introduced Zen to the West, and who influenced whole generations of Buddhists; Prof. Nicholas Berdyaev, the eminent philosopher, and Dr S Radhakrishnan, the Vedantin scholar who was later to become President of India. There were also many other speakers, each one an expert in his own field. The records that I have seen do not show that there were any women speakers – a sign of the times – though there were two women asked to chair sessions, one of whom, Dame Elizabeth Cadbury, was a Quaker. She also gave a great deal of support to Sir Francis in the early days of the WCF. It was recognised that each participant had a contribution to make, and it was also emphasised that the purpose was not to seek to change anybody's religion, but to promote deeper understanding. However, looking back, the chief impact was not found in the Congress itself, but in the various organisations that grew out of it and carried on the work. The principle one – which is still active today – took for its name the title 'World Congress of Faiths'.[6]

There have been other events that have added to our understanding of the world as one. In 1969, the first manned landing on the moon and the resulting photographs of the earth provided an icon of oneness which is still reverberating into the 21st century. Some years later in 1987, came the founding of the Interfaith Network for the UK, and the establishment of local Interfaith Councils which paralleled the work of local ecumenical groups which had been in existence for some years. Many Quaker meetings and individuals contributed to both of these, and continue to do so.

In addition to these specific events, the growing phenomenon of international and inter-disciplinary publishing has ensured that those who wish to share the spiritual teachings of others have access to relevant material. Much is now available in translation, and in many different versions. For example, let us take the teachings of Taoism. Though it is one of the less organised religions, its major writing, the *Tao Teh Ching*, is among the most translated books in the world. It is also one which has probably the greatest number of commentaries. On my own bookshelves (and I must confess a deep personal interest) there are over 50 translations, each containing a commentary, ranging from the earliest (dated 1894) to one published this year. Approaches range from strictly academic translations by notable sinologists, to translations by language teachers, poets, psychologists, martial artists and healers. Writers from many other faiths have acknowledged its influence, including Jews, Christians and Buddhists. Translations from *The Qur'an, The Bhagavad Gita, The Lotus Sutra* and other well-known world scriptures may not be so numerous, but there are more than enough to interest the seeker and give opportunities for reading, study and comparison.

This sharing of information is likely to become more prevalent with the increase in Internet activity. The concept of cyberspace allows the influence of all kinds of spiritual traditions, beliefs and practices to permeate the consciousness of seekers who use it. In the paradox that here is something that is real, yet does not have an existence, it is in itself close to the mystical reality behind religion. Already there are thousands of websites on all kinds of religious and New Age teachings ranging from the academic to the essentially practical, and the doctrinal to the esoteric and mystical. There is little excuse – other than prejudice – for anyone to be able to say that they are unable to find out what the various faiths think about themselves. However, the sheer quantity of information and ideas is literally mind-boggling, and may yet prove to be too much for individuals to cope with.

This whole idea of shared spirituality is a phenomenon of this century, and will probably be even more significant in the new millennium. It is often criticised as being syncretism, or derogatively called "supermarket spirituality"; each person being able to wander through life collecting those items which seem helpful to them. There is in fact nothing wrong with this, provided those items which are right for oneself are not assumed to be right for all. We each have to live our own lives, and we cannot live the lives of others, as they cannot live ours. We have to find those spiritual practices which are the right ones for us, and are most helpful in the particular places and states in which we find ourselves. It is helpful to recognise that these will change as we grow. St Paul referred to this when he talked about being a child, and being happy with those things that were childish. Then we grow up, though we must not do so to the extent that we forget the teaching of Jesus, who told us that unless we can be "as little children", then we will not enter the Kingdom of Heaven.

Of course, religion is not *just* a matter of individual preference. There are many factors which decide our religious pathway. The main ones are the circumstances of our birth, the teachings received in our early years (which can either keep us within a particular faith, or cause us to seek elsewhere) and the need for community. The essence of community is spiritual friendship. There is a story about Ananda, the beloved disciple and personal attendant of the Buddha. Because Ananda was so busy serving the Buddha, he tended to miss some of the vital teachings, and it is said that he did not receive the enlightenment experience which came to most of the other immediate disciples through listening to the teachings of the Buddha. Ananda had to find his own way to enlightenment by a slower and more spasmodic route, and this is recorded in a number of stories which illustrate the stages of his discovery. (Ananda is, of course, "Everyman", and so his discoveries are often more helpful to ordinary people than the intuitive and philosophical heights exhibited by some others.) One day Ananda came to the Buddha and spoke of his discovery of spiritual friendship, saying, "Lord, I have discovered that spiritual friendship is half the spiritual life". "Say not so, Ananda", responded the Buddha. "Say rather that spiritual friendship is the whole of the spiritual life!"

It is this sense of spiritual friendship or community that is another vital factor in our choice of a religious faith. We join a religious body – usually with its church, temple or other meeting place – because we find there other people who are at similar stages on the spiritual path, or who have been that way before, and are able to help us. There is always a social aspect to religion. Few of us are natural hermits who feel happiest walking the spiritual path on our own, and even hermits usually have those they can turn to at time of difficulty, such as a spiritual director or guru. Hermits also have contact with those who seek them out for their presumed wisdom and spiritual attainments.

Quakers have always had a certain way of dealing with their Christian faith which has allowed them to be, as *Advices and Queries* #7 tells us, "Open to Fresh Light from wherever it may come". Early Friends had a very clear vision. They were not presenting anything new. What they were doing was recovering the original teachings of Jesus, before these were corrupted by the politics and power-seeking of the Church, and then trying to live by them. This, they felt, allowed them to discover the same approach to the world that Jesus had. It also changed their attitude to the person of Jesus, and to God. The language of their spirituality was new, because it was that which came from the awareness that "Christ [was] come to teach his people himself".[7] It was most definitely Christian, but

4

was often not recognised as such by those who heard it. That which it represented was as old as humanity itself, and could thus be said to be truly universal.

Because of this, it was inevitable that Quakerism would be open to change and growth over the more than three hundred years of its existence. Quakerism in the twentieth century could not be the same as it was in the seventeenth, eighteenth, nineteenth centuries, or even the early part of the twentieth century. That it is still recognisably Quakerism is because, in addition to being open to change, the essential testimonies and the power of silent worship are still there, even though they too have adapted in response to the needs of the world in which we live.

Quakers are a society of *friends*. For us, therefore, spiritual friendship is, if not the whole story, then a very significant part of our spiritual lives. Most of us are Friends either because we were born into the Society, or because we have left some other branch of the Christian faith because we could not in conscience say that we accepted those things which we were expected to believe – and sometimes recite – in order to remain a member of that particular church. We may have left another church over some matter of principle, such as the support of war or violence, or the perceived indoctrination of children. We come to a Friends meeting, and there we find a group of people with whom we can agree, not on everything, but on those matters which are dearest to us, or perhaps even on the lack of a need for agreement. The meeting becomes our home, and the members our new family.

Now all this is perfectly normal and natural, but, as well as its joys, it also has its dangers. These may arise – just as they did in creedal churches – if we start to disagree with some or even all of the meeting on a particular issue. Peer pressure is a very real problem within religion, and it becomes even more of one if we are led to take the extreme step of leaving a church or other religious body. This is, in fact, one of the accusations levelled at many of the new religions, but it applies just as well to the old ones. How do we leave somewhere when all – or at least many – of our friends and companions on the spiritual path are still 'within the fold'? How do we speak out, even among such a liberal body as Friends, when we disagree with something that the organisation as a whole has agreed to, but which every fibre of our being and our conscience says is wrong for us?

All this encapsulates one of the major problems of interfaith dialogue; that of organisations, and all that goes with them, such as property, united action or belief, and authoritarianism. It is this which has been one of the major obstacles to Quaker interfaith work. While individual Friends have found it easy to share with those of other faiths, it has usually been the

5

organisations which have created barriers. This is true not only among Friends, but within organised religion in general.

There is a story – found in many different versions – of God and the Devil who are standing at a street corner, when they see someone ahead of them bend down and pick up something bright and shining. "Look", says God, "that person has just found some Truth. Aren't you worried?" "No!" replies the Devil, "not in the least. You see, I'm going to help them organise it".

In writing this book, I have come again and again to the realisation that organisations can be either a blessing or a curse. Within Quaker circles, we have many levels of organisation, because most of our work is initiated and supported within a committee structure. This also has strengths and weaknesses. Its strength is that it provides us with a way in which the leadings of an individual can be tested to see if they lead to something that is felt to be the will of God for the Society as a whole. When this works, it is one of the most beautiful processes, inspiring and empowering. There are occasions, however, when the inspirations of an individual Friend may be felt to be too far outside the prevailing views, and too risky to involve Friends as a whole. Luckily, there are Friends who are clear that the the Spirit is stronger than the dead weight of organisation, and they are led forward to allow the Spirit to work.

Over the years, this determination to listen to the leadings of the Spirit has led to many initiatives which have added significantly to the sum total of interfaith dialogue in the world. The story of Quaker interfaith work is mostly the story of such individuals, sometimes supported by their meetings from the beginning, sometimes working alone and only approved later, while a few are still not fully appreciated. None-the-less, for their numbers and their quiet way of working, Quakers have made very significant contributions to the field of interfaith dialogue.

When any venture begins to take shape, it is interesting to look back and observe the time when it seems to take on a life of its own. In Quaker terms, there is a time when it becomes clear that a project is the result of a real concern, and one becomes aware that the Spirit which motivated it in the first place is That which will help to see it through. When we start on such a venture, we often have fixed ideas as to the form that it should take. This is not necessarily right, and we have to be open to allow the Spirit to move. Then the final result can often be very different and much more exciting than we had envisaged.

This is what happened with this book. The original idea for it came from the work of the Friends Interfaith Group which Margot Tennyson and I founded way back in 1978. We had always felt the need for some publications which would highlight the unique contributions that Quakers could make to Interfaith dialogue. One result was the booklet *Three Spiritual Journeys*, which the FIFG published in 1984, and which contained three of the talks which the FIFG sponsored at London Yearly Meeting (now Britain YM). Then there was Margot's book, *Friends and Other Faiths*, which was published by QHS in 1992. It outlined many of the ways in which Friends had become involved in this field, and gave some accounts of Margot's own varied experiences. It also pointed Friends towards future possibilities.

As the teachings and practices of other faith traditions became increasingly important to individual Friends, this degree of personal involvement raised more questions, and something else was needed. Margot was asked to write another book on the subject, taking Friends on from 1992, looking at the problems that had arisen and the benefits that many Friends had found. Unfortunately, due to ill-health, she was unable to write it, and I was asked to do so. After quite a bit of research, I began to see three distinct areas that needed to be addressed.

The first was to briefly recap some of the facts in *Friends and Other Faiths*, to add other material that – for one reason or another – had not found its way into that book, and to talk about some of the work that Friends had been involved in since 1992. It has always been the case that Quaker involvement in this field, as with so many others, is the result of concerns felt by individual Friends. This has meant that much of the work has been local, carried on in the usual quiet Quaker fashion, without publicity, and with very few people, outside those directly involved, knowing anything about the results. This is good, and it will, I think, always be the Quaker way. It means that sensitive issues can be covered away from the glare of media attention. A result of this is that those involved feel able to deal with issues that they could not otherwise tackle. It does however, have a certain disadvantage in that others in the field may feel isolated.

Quakers, and in particular Britain Yearly Meeting, have made considerable progress in this field over the last 25 years. In 1994 Meeting for Sufferings agreed to have an official body to work on interfaith matters, and the work was passed to the Committee on Christian Relationships, which later became the Quaker Committee for Christian and Inter-faith Relationships (CIR). This body is still continuing interfaith work on behalf of the Yearly Meeting. The Friends Interfaith Group was laid down at this point, as it became clear that we had achieved most of the aims for which it was set up, and core members felt that they were being led to work in other areas.

The second thread of this book is to highlight some of the lesser-known aspects of Quaker involvement in the area of interfaith matters. Some of these have been well documented elsewhere, but are little-known to Friends in general. Others, such as the Pendle Hill Quaker Study Center in the USA, are well-known in their own right, but their contribution to the interfaith field has not be emphasised, particularly in the UK. Many of their courses and pamphlets have been oriented towards the field of interfaith studies, and they have had a great influence in the field, not least by the publication of Douglas Steere's pamphlet, *Mutual Irradiation*. Similarly, some of the courses held at Charney Manor, the Quaker conference and retreat centre in Oxfordshire, have been concerned with meeting the needs of British Friends whose personal journeys have included influence and practices drawn from other faiths. They have also provided a space where Friends who sometimes feel isolated in their meetings, are able to discuss their problems and their joys with others who have had the same experience.

Other influences have come from the writing of a single book. A good example is the work of the American Friend, Bradford Smith, whose book, *Meditation the Inward Art* is hardly ever mentioned when Friends get together to discuss the subject of meditation, for the sad reason that few of them have ever seen a copy or know of its existence. I think it is an absolute gem, and, as mentioned in the acknowledgements, it has been a great influence on me. It was published in the UK in 1964 by George Allen and Unwin, but sadly, was never reprinted.

Also, looking at the influence of books, Sessions of York have recently published a number of works by and about Marjorie Sykes, who was involved with almost every aspect of Quaker interfaith work in India. These show aspects of her inner life which, though within the Quaker tradition, was deeply influenced by the spirituality of India, in particular Mahatma Gandhi and Rabindranath Tagore.

The third, and, for me, the principle reason for writing this book, is to try to answer some of the questions that have been raised by the increasing influence of other faith traditions on the spiritual lives of many Friends. This growing interest in the teachings and practices of other faiths is in some ways similar to the increasing involvement of Quakers in the arts as ways of spiritual expression. Early Friends were very much opposed to the arts, and saw them as distractions to the spiritual life. Members who practised them were even disowned, and there is at least one case of musicians publicly burning their instruments after they became Quakers. In modern times, Friends have realised that the arts are a valid form of spiritual language, and a number of Quaker poets, composers and painters – as well as a number of Friends in various aspects of the performing arts – have become names that are nationally recognised.

As time goes by, more and more Friends find that the writings and the practices of other faith traditions become important to them. Whether it is the teachings about God found in Hinduism, Judaism or Islam; those on non-violence from the Hindu and Buddhist traditions; teachings on meditation from Zen Roshis or Yogic Gurus; and even the influence of the Christian mystics, the language of other traditions has permeated our Western culture; and Friends are not immune. An example is the *Tao Teh Ching* which was only known by a few enthusiasts 25 years ago. In recent times it has influenced people as diverse as those concerned with new business methods, with healing, or even those who have been brought up on the magic of Winnie-the-Pooh. It has also inspired at least one Quaker to publish a translation.

Such increasing influence has advantages and disadvantages. Among the advantages are the provision of methods – for those who need them – of stilling the mind and finding inner peace, and making these available to the general public. An example is *The Little Book of Calm*, a small book on relaxation and meditation that found a place in the best-seller lists for many weeks. Such methods can and do complement the Quaker traditions of silent meeting, and the awareness of the presence of God in our everyday lives. Another joy is the discovery of new forms of language which some feel expresses their spiritual experience more fully than that of the Bible or of traditional Quakerism. The principle danger is that some Friends and Attenders get so carried away by these new discoveries that they sometimes completely reject traditional Quaker language and practices, thereby losing the roots and fruits of a tradition that has worked well for many thousands of people for over 300 years.

A further problem is caused by making comparisons between various teachings and practices. When we are faced with a teaching or practice that works for us, and then with another from a different source which uses different language, it can cause confusion. A good example is the Quaker tradition of waiting on God (where God is known as a living and inspiring Presence) contrasted with the Buddhist tradition of teaching meditation in a way that has no reference to God, and in fact may actively discourage mention of Him.[8] Such a paradox provokes and thus stimulates the reasoning mind. This has caused great confusion for some Friends, leading to a state of mind that is too restless to enable them to find the Presence of God in Meeting, and which also inhibits their practice of meditation.

In my years of working with Friends in this field, and in facilitating conferences at Charney Manor and elsewhere, I have had to try to help many Friends with such difficulties. All I could do is to share what I have discovered for myself in such circumstances, and I hope it has been helpful. This is all I can do in this part of the book. Actually, the essence of what I have discovered is twofold, and can be put into a few words. If we seek the Silence *first*, in whatever way seems right for us, then as the silence deepens there will be a letting-go of concepts, and the discovery of harmony in the Spirit. This seems to me to be an example of what Jesus meant when he said, "Seek first the Kingdom of God, and all else will be added". The corollary to this is that, in the spiritual life, apparent opposites are reconciled. This may be why Jesus told us, "Judge not"[9] and the Buddhist Hsin Hsin Ming, one of my favourite scriptures, says,

The Perfect Way knows no difficulties,
Except that it refuses to make preferences; ...[10]

Although the essence can be told in a few simple words, simple does not mean easy. I cannot claim that I always, or even often, remember that this is the way out. All I can say is that, when I do remember, it works for me. Then I find a clarity in which all my thinking and my reasoning will never find, and harmony is restored to situations in most unexpected ways. Thus, this art of seeking stillness as the first response is not only a form of meditation; it is also a form of prayer. And it is prayer, silence and meditation that is the key to the interfaith work that has been done over the last twenty-five years. If it continues to work for those who want to try it, then I will feel that part of the purpose in writing this book has been fulfilled.

CHAPTER 1

There is a Principle!

"THERE IS A PRINCIPLE..." This wonderful affirmation of John Woolman quoted at the beginning of the book has been an inspiration to the many Friends who have worked and are still working in the field of interfaith sharing. For over 300 years, Quakers have waited in silence in order that the nature of this Principle might be revealed. It is not unique to Friends. There are many people of other faiths who similarly wait in silence – either in groups or on their own – to discover this Principle or Divine Essence as a living force in their lives. So it is not only a *Quaker* Principle.

John Woolman is very clear that this Pure Principle is placed within the human mind. Christians call it "The Mind that was in Christ Jesus", or "The Cosmic Christ". In Buddhism, it is the "Unborn Buddha Mind" or our "Original Face". In Hinduism, it is the *Atman*, in the sense of the Self that is One with God. In China, it was known as the Tao, while the other monotheistic religions speak of "the Soul" or "the Spirit" or use phrases similar to the Quaker term "That of God".

In the early days of Quakerism, most spiritual experience was expressed in the language of the Bible. Quakers expanded the language of spiritual experience by using terms such as "the Inward Light", "the Seed" or "the Leaven". Today, we have access to a great variety of spiritual language. There are many translations of the Bible, from the King James to the most modern versions. We have discovered lost scriptures that were a part of the Gnostic tradition and which were omitted from the canonical Bible. The majority of the scriptures of the world's religions have now been translated into English, and are also freely available to us. There are also the writings of mystics and poets, not only from the European traditions, but also from many other faiths and cultures. Likewise, the works of philosophers and scientists spanning more than a thousand years are also published in book form.

Quakerism is a religion of experience. Experience is best expressed in silence, but human beings also have a need to express it in words. The world's mystics – including Quakers – show us the silence that is behind the words, but they also felt the need to use language. Mystical experience inevitably leads to an expansion of the language that is used to express it. Quakers have always been interested in expanding the language of the spirit. It is no wonder that today many Friends have turned to the *Upanishads, Tao Teh Ching*, the *Qur'an*, the *Dhammapada* and other scriptures, to see if their language might be more helpful in describing the experience that is essentially beyond words, but which we find in a gathered Quaker Meeting and in contemplation of the Inward Light.

There is also another dimension that needs to be considered. Christianity is very good at describing and making real the presence of a Personal God. However, science increasingly shows us an expanding universe, and the media makes us aware of a world in which there are many problems such as suffering, war, hunger and natural disasters. The modern mind is no longer satisfied to see these as the will of a God who is seen as fickle and discriminatory. Quakers, in our meetings for worship, experience the Presence of God as a living reality, but many find it hard to say whether this Presence was personal or impersonal. Whichever it is, we are mostly happy to affirm that we experience this Presence as Love. So how do we reconcile this universal Love with the suffering and tragedies of a changing world? This is the dilemma facing Friends today, and, because the language of the Bible is mostly personal, it provides another reason to look elsewhere for suitable language to describe our experience.

None of this denies the Christian roots of the Quaker tradition. What it does do is to emphasise the special approach which sees the 'Inward Light' or 'That of God' as the final guide in spiritual matters. It is no wonder that many Friends feel in harmony with the Buddha, who, when he was speaking to the *Kalama* people in a discourse that has been called the first example of spiritual free enquiry, told them not to accept anything just because it has been said by a teacher, even the Buddha himself, or because it had been written in a holy book.

The *Advices and Queries* say something similar, though in different words.

> Take heed, dear Friends, to the promptings of love and truth in your hearts. Trust them as the leadings of God whose Light shows us our Darkness, and brings us to new life (A & Q #1).

> Be aware of the Spirit of God at work in the ordinary activities and experience of your daily life... Are you open to new light, from whatever source it may come? Do you approach new ideas with discernment? (A & Q #7).

If it is true, if we really do believe that there is "That of God" in everyone, then we may reasonably expect this Divine Essence to be recognised widely. In this recognition that we can find Peace in ourselves, in others, and in the world. This is the Peace that Christ told us He gave freely and without condition, in which we can discover, here and now, the Kingdom of Heaven which is often spoken of as a coming event. If we are secure in our Christian roots, then we will be able to look at other forms of language, and find the Divine aspect that we call Christ in them, even if they come from sources other than the Bible. One of the great discoveries of early Friends was that Christ, in coming to teach His people Himself, did not only speak in Biblical language, or in the traditional words of the church.

This is the real meaning of and justification for interfaith work. It is what Douglas Steere calls "Mutual Irradiation". His Pendle Hill Pamphlet of the same name has been a major source of inspiration to Friends working in this field. When we acknowledge the Light of the Spirit shining freely, without hindrance, through all the parts of the universe including ourselves, then interfaith studies are not purely of academic interest, nor even attempts at finding language which comes close to expressing our experience. They become true prayer, which lifts up all creation to a higher level.

Inspiring though this view of interfaith relations may be, it is not the whole of the story. Nor is the adoption of a new language, however sublime, always the complete answer. Friends are also deeply concerned for peace in the world, and for harmony in the area of community relations. Quakers have become known for their mediation skills, and for their ability and willingness to listen impartially. Many disputes in terms of race or nationality also have a religious dimension. Much of this work that Friends are quietly getting on with has been inspired by the example of Mahatma Gandhi, who was involved with Friends in India.

There has been an interfaith dimension to much of Quaker peace work in various parts of the world. Friends have found that they have to be clear in their own minds that they are following a genuine concern to assist the peace process, and a part of this is a real need to understand the faith and practices of the antagonists. The combination of these and the willingness to listen without judgement, has often been the key to being able to suggest ways in which the parties might talk to each other. If Friends did not believe that there was something of God in people of all faiths and none, they would not be able to adopt this open attitude.

Some of the unsung work in which Quakers have been involved has been in helping various religious groups to understand and accept each other. Work in this country between Jewish and Muslim communities, and also between Hindus, Muslims and Sikhs has often been facilitated because there has been a Quaker Meeting House available, as well as Friends who were prepared to listen. Quakers have become known and accepted for their work in Northern Ireland, where, although they come from a Protestant non-conformist background, they are seen by some of the parties as being "neither Catholic nor Protestant", and thus able to listen and work with both sides of the divide.

In comparatively small local disputes, Friends are involved in mediation, and some of this work revolves around religious issues. I have discovered that most of the Quakers involved do not want their work publicised, for fear they might be thought to be doing it in order to gain converts to Quakerism. I have respected their wishes. Quaker meeting houses are often made available to local groups who have no temple or other place of worship of their own, and this is welcomed because the meeting houses have no overt religious symbols. Friends are appreciated for this because, although recognised as part of the Christian community, they are seen to have a special attitude towards other faith communities. This can apply even when the Friends concerned are not particularly concerned with interfaith issues in the general sense.

In all these approaches we see the Spirit moving. Friends become aware of a situation, but are unsure what to do about it. The problem may be taken to the Meeting for Business, or a special Meeting for Clearness may be held. I have experienced such meetings. The question is taken into the silence and Friends wait to see what inspiration will come. As a possible solution is revealed, so the means to adopt it also becomes clear. We know for ourselves what George Fox meant when he spoke of "the Power of the Lord being over all". Events unfold in ways that we could never have planned, and people come forward from outside the meeting to volunteer for tasks that were their speciality.

✡ ☦ ☾ ✷ ☯ ✺ ॐ

I have already referred briefly to the confusion that can arise when Friends discover other ways of approaching God, or of quieting what has been referred to as "The Monkey Mind". Some may have found most of what they need in the meeting for worship, but discover that there is still something missing. They may find Quaker worship a beautiful experience, but have great difficulty in centring down in meeting. Discovering the Buddhist way of observing the breath to still the mind, or being shown how to use a mantra in meditation, they find that these things work for them. They think of using them in meeting, only to be firmly told by elders that meeting is not the same as meditation, and that they should not be doing this. This causes confusion. This confusion is one of the principle reasons for this book, and we need to accept that it is a normal state for the seeking mind.

The questions that I have been asked by confused Friends over the past twenty or so years have been one of my key inspirations in writing. I do not claim to know all the answers. I do not even claim to know all the

14

questions. But where I have been able to make suggestions which have been found helpful, or where Friends have found the answers for themselves, and have come back and told me of their discoveries, these are the things that I would like to share with you. In the end, the answers will come from the guidance that each of us has available from within. All that I can share are suggestions, but they are suggestions that have arisen out of somebody's experience.

Perhaps it might be helpful to start by sharing a little of my own experience. Some of it I have written elsewhere. But it seems to me that I cannot fully explain my involvement with Friends and their interfaith work without the reader knowing where I have come from. We are all influenced by the experiences of our lives in both the spiritual and material dimensions, even if we do try to blend the two. It is important that we recognise that our opinions are shaped by these events, and an awareness of this leads us to an holistic acceptance of who and what we are.

I think I became a Quaker by accident. Certainly I thought it was an accident for many years. But the more I discover about the role of the Inward Light in guiding a person's life – even if they are not aware of it – the more I wonder what was really going on, and how I came to be in a Quaker meeting in the first place. Looking back, I can see a pattern of which I was quite unaware at the time. Had it not been so, I would probably not have ended up working at Friends House for the best part of eighteen years, or met Margot Tennyson. I would almost certainly not have become involved with the founding of the Friends Interfaith Group, and had the wonderful blending of influences that has led me to being asked to write this book.

I was born and brought up as a Roman Catholic, and it was thought by all concerned – including myself – that I was going to be a priest. However, I had trouble with the idea of faith, something that has stayed with me all my life. There are many things that I believe, some that I can say I know, and many things and people that I trust. But I do not know any of this as 'faith', though others tell me that it is so. Anyway, this problem with faith led me to ask many questions, so many that it was decided that I was unsuitable for the priesthood, a view that I was beginning to share. Eventually it led to my leaving that church. I will always be grateful to it for the basic religious up-bringing that it gave me, for the love of early music and chanting that is still with me, and for giving me things to question.

I immersed myself in left-wing politics for a while, looking round – though not obviously – for an alternative philosophy. I explored various other branches of Christianity, Yoga, Spiritualism and Theosophy, but did not feel completely at home anywhere. Eventually, I went to a meeting of the local Young Socialists, only to find that I had turned up on the wrong day, and there was a Buddhist monk speaking to a group about the *Kalama Sutta*, where the Buddha advises the seekers from the *Kalamas* to put their own experience before that of any authority. I had discovered Buddhism, and it was just what I needed. I joined the local group, and learned to meditate.

After I had been with this Buddhist group for about two years it folded, as the chairman was moving and the secretary died. I felt lost. I missed the meditation, and also the companionship of the other members. Somebody told me; "If you want a quiet place to meditate, go to the Quakers. They have an hour's meditation on a Sunday morning". I went, and immediately felt at home, though this was probably because, at the time I joined it, that particular meeting was almost entirely silent. It was not until much later that I discovered that this was not always the case. It was quite a shock when someone first stood and spoke in ministry.

But that shock decided me. I realised that if I were to stay there I needed to know much more about these people, and explore what was actually going on. I took my usual path. I read, and I asked questions about the things that I did not find clear in the books. I discovered that Quakers believed in God, but that it was not the God of orthodox Christian theology, distant and apart from us. They believed in "that of God" within each person, and in direct access for each person. They met in a silent group, not for meditation of a personal kind, but because the Quaker experience is that this is the best way to discover the presence of God. In the silence, they said, God's voice can be heard.

I had discovered something that is still important for me. If I am to have a religion, then it must be a practical one; one which brings inner peace in the here and now. Quakers shared with the Buddhists an inner peace and tranquillity, and the belief in peace and non-violence which was one of the things that had first attracted me to Buddhism. They also had a compassionate restlessness towards the suffering of the world. Both Buddhism and Quakerism are experiential; they value a person's experiences, and so for me the progression from one to another seemed to happen naturally.

Later I realised that I had not left behind my Roman Catholic upbringing, and that I did not cease to be a Buddhist when I encountered – and eventually joined – the Quakers. I see myself as both a Quaker and a Buddhist. And, because the form of Buddhism to which I was eventually attracted did not have an established centre in this country, I am profoundly grateful to Friends for providing the sense of 'Sangha' (religious community) which is so essential to Buddhism. But I also respect the Christian basis of Friends, and can accept the advice which tells us that Quakerism is "...rooted in Christianity and has always found inspiration in the life and teachings of Jesus". (A & Q #4) It was this that enabled me to apply for membership. I made no secret of my Buddhism when I was visited, but I made it clear that I respected the Christian roots of Quakerism, and that I did find the life and teachings of Jesus an inspiration, even if not the only one. This must have been found satisfactory, because I was accepted into membership.

I started this section by referring to the confusion that can be caused when a seeker discovers by experience that there is not just a single way to the Truth. I have lived though that confusion. I am now certain in my own mind that if Gautama Buddha and Jesus Christ (or indeed, any other of the founders of world religions) were to meet, there would be no disagreement between them. I suspect that they would share the deepest silence, and then might laugh and exchange stories. They might even cry together. They probably would not talk about religion. Certainly they would not get involved in any kind of debate as to the relative merits of the State of Nirvana or the Kingdom of Heaven.

We are told by those who wish to discourage the study of other faith traditions that there can be no real meeting place with Christianity, and that the Christian Heaven is the only place that the 'saved' soul will go. The fact that Buddhists do not have a concept of a 'soul' in the Christian sense only adds fuel to the fire.

I am convinced that only a person who has reached Nirvana on the Buddhist path, and has been fully saved by the Christian, is the one who might be able to tell us conclusively that they are different. And I am not sure that such people exist, and I suspect that if they do, they would not want to make such a categorical statement. Buddha certainly had no knowledge of the Christian way, and while some knowledge of Buddhism might have reached first century Israel, and there is a tradition that Jesus visited India before his public ministry commenced, there is no firm evidence of any direct influence. There are, however, many parallel sayings, which indicate that the high state of the two religious founders may not have been far apart. [11]

I quote the relationship between Christianity and Buddhism because this is the area where I have most experience. I will say more about this in Chapter 8. But I have also found great harmony between the Quaker Way and the mystical aspects of most of the major religions. And I know that many Friends have found the same.

It is conclusions such as this that have influenced me to work in the field of interfaith understanding. They have grown out of a need in my own life, and, talking with other Friends, I find similar needs and responses.

CHAPTER 2

In the beginning

THERE IS EVIDENCE that, from the earliest times, Quakers had some knowledge of other faiths and their impact upon the world. They knew the Jewish scriptures because of their familiarity with the Old Testament. It is possible that they had knowledge of other traditions. Even if this was not so, it is clear from writings of some early Friends that Quakers had an openness to traditions such as those of the Native Americans in a way that was not shared by most of their European Christian contemporaries.

The seventeenth century was in some ways like our own, and in many ways very different. The power of the monarch, and that of the church, were absolute in the lives of ordinary people. Everyone was expected to accept the Christian faith as the only right one, and, in England, only one form of that faith was permitted. This was usually the faith of the monarch, and dissent was treason. Non-comformity led to persecution. However, the more those in power try to suppress discussion, particularly about religion, the more discussion takes place. So it was that, in spite of heavy persecution, groups of dissenters arose on all sides.

It must have seemed to the orthodox Christians – who would have been mostly Anglicans – that Quakers were introducing ideas that were far outside the Christian tradition. Quakers themselves felt that they were only going back to the beliefs and practices of the early church, or as they would have said, primitive Christianity. Actually, within the Protestant and Catholic traditions there were mystics who had similarly experienced the Light of Christ within as a reality, though they were usually content to write and speak about it within the language and structure of their church. Indeed, it could have been – and often was – dangerous to do otherwise.

It is difficult to give an idea of the origins of Quakerism in a few paragraphs. Probably most readers will know more about them than I do. There were many people involved, from differing levels of society. Though as a specific movement it started around the mid-seventeenth century, the famous Quaker historian, Rufus Jones (who was a mystic himself) feels Quakerism to be a part of the stream of mysticism which started with Dionysius, and included Jacob Boehme, St Francis of Assisi, Meister Eckhart and The Friends of God. There may or may not have been physical contact with these ideas, but the essence of their teachings and practices was, so to speak 'in the air'. It arose out of the search for religious experience that was true to the Holy Spirit. I believe that this Spirit was moving in many different ways at that time.

George Fox

George Fox is often quoted as the 'founder' of Quakerism. We know that he was by no means the only founder, but his influence was so great that we sometimes find difficulty in explaining why we do not see him as our "founder" in the sense that the term is usually used. Fox's teaching, charisma, spiritual and other gifts were vital to the formation of Quakerism as a movement, but there were many others whose contribution was equally valuable. It was truly a movement of the Spirit. When George Fox had his own personal revelation and met others who were similarly searching, there was a new beginning. In reality, the founder of Quakerism and of all true movements of the Spirit is That of God which we call "The Inward Light", and is known by many other names. One thing Quakers have found is that It has to be discovered anew in each generation.

George Fox was a born seeker. Experiencing one crisis after another, he always sought the direct experience of the Spirit, only later finding the words which would express it to others. He was prepared to wrestle with earthly and other-worldly powers and to question anyone he thought might have answers, in order to find peace of mind. Eventually, he had the much-quoted spiritual experience in which he heard a voice tell him, "There is one, even Christ Jesus, that can speak to thy condition"[12] and he experienced an inner power and healing. He wandered around the country, getting into trouble for interrupting sermons, debating with all who would do so, but all the time meeting those who would later be known as 'The Valiant Sixty', the nucleus of the Quaker movement. Many were so inspired by Fox's preaching, that they had an on the spot 'conversion' or even an 'enlightenment' experience.

George Fox was physically very strong, and this enabled him to survive the rigours of constant travelling and the traumas of imprisonment. He also felt that he was upheld in all that he did by the Spirit of Christ which guided him in his ministry. He was known to be absolutely honest in all that he did or said. He hated hypocrisy of every kind, and exposed it wherever he could. Above all, he was a powerful and charismatic mystic with outstanding organising ability, who was able to project his vision and inspire others to find theirs. In some ways, he still inspires Friends through his *Journal* and other writings. William Penn said of him, "He was an original, being no man's copy"[13] George Fox was absolutely clear in his own mind that "Christ is come to teach His people himself",[14] and that this was nothing less than the restoration of the teachings and practices of the early Christian church.

George Fox had an excellent memory, and a great knowledge of the Bible. He had studied the words contained within it hoping to find that which would satisfy his deep spiritual yearning. Instead, he was later able to find within that book the experiences of other prophets and mystics which enabled him to verify his own. This knowledge, coupled with his own spiritual insight, enabled him to argue with others who were far more theologically qualified than himself, but often did not have the experience of the Divine. Indeed, Fox's personal guidance was such that it often enabled him to discern when a person, whether or not within holy orders, had a similar awareness of the immanence of the Spirit.

It has also emerged in recent times that George Fox had a knowledge of the Qur'an. In a recent issue of the *Journal of the Friends Historical Society* there is an article by N I Matar entitled 'Some Notes on George Fox and Islam', in which the writer reveals that Fox acquired a copy of *The Qur'an* in the 1649 translation by Alexander Ross, and that he soon became familiar enough to be able to use and quote accurately from it, citing chapter and verse. Although Fox's main purpose was to use it to help in converting the Muslims, which was something that few others – even Quakers – thought about doing, he was also able to use it to plead for better treatment of Quaker and other Christian pilgrims who had been captured by the Muslims. He pointed out that the physical and sexual abuse of them by their captors was against "the law of the great god, and your own *Alcoran* (sic)".

In these arguments, Fox was not seeking to convert the Muslim Sultan, but used the authority of *The Qur'an* to shame him into ordering more humane treatment of the captives. On other occasions, he was able to use the Muslim respect for Jesus and the Old Testament prophets as discussion points, and to quote similar verses from *The Qur'an* together with the Gospels and other biblical texts.[15]

William Penn

William Penn was in many ways very different from George Fox. Born into the nobility, he was still a seeker, who found his revelation in the Quaker message. When Penn came to America, he showed a deep humility in his dealings with the Native American tribes. Although they did not have written scriptures to refer to, Penn was able to discern that they:

...Owned a superior power, and [he] asked the interpreter what their notion was of God in their own way. The interpreter showed, by making several circles on the ground with his staff, till he reduced the last into a small circumference, and placed, as he said, by way of representation, The Great Man (as they termed him) in the middle circle, so that he could see over all the other circles, which included the earth. (From: *Some Accounts of the Religious Society of Friends Towards the Indian Tribes*, page 61)[16]

His mystical insights inspired him in his work for the betterment of the world in which he lived, and this is shown in a willingness to listen and learn, even from non-Christians. This is not strange to Friends. We know of this attitude through one of his statements which has been a principle inspiration to Friends working in the field of interfaith relations, and which finds a place in Quaker Faith and Practice.

The humble, meek, merciful, just, pious and devout souls are everywhere of one religion; and when death has taken off the mask they will know one another, though the diverse liveries they wear here makes them strangers. This world is a form; our bodies are forms; and no visible acts of devotion can be without forms. Yet the less form in religion, the better, since God is a Spirit; for the more mental our worship, the more suitable to the language of the Spirit. (QFP 19:28)

James Nayler

Among early Friends, the name of James Nayler is well known, though often for the wrong reasons. Nayler was tried for blasphemy because it was said that, in his imitation of Jesus's ride into Jerusalem, he had claimed to be Christ. It is true that there were all the outward signs, and also that some of his followers were carried away by the scene. It may also be true that Nayler identified himself with Jesus as he was acting out the ride. However, this does not mean blasphemy. A knowledge of other faith traditions gives us an insight into Nayler's actions which is not readily apparent from other sources.

I feel certain that James Nayler was an ecstatic mystic; one who identifies himself totally with the form of God that he worships. Had he been, for example, a Hindu, there would have been no problem. Sri Chaitanya and many other of Hinduism's greatest saints performed similar pageants where they became – for a while – the form of God that they were portraying. Indeed, such an ability is considered one of the signs of high spiritual attainment within Hinduism, and the ecstatic saint is considered to have all the powers of the God or Goddess, and to be able to convey blessings, and bring about healings and answers to prayers. Known in Sanskrit as *Bhava*, there are several attitudes that the *bhakti* or devotee may adopt towards his or her chosen deity. These include a serene friendship, the

21

attitude of a parent or child, of a servant towards a master, or the acting out of a scene in the life of the Divine Person, just as Nayler did.

Ecstatic mysticism is not unknown in Christianity. The most well-known examples are those of the stigmatics, whose devotion to the form of Christ crucified leads them to manifest the marks of His crucifixion on their own bodies. That these marks may not be accurate to what is now known about crucifixion is not the point (e.g. there may be holes in the palms of the hands, which – it is now generally agreed – would not actually support a hanging body) . The stigmatic's devotion is to a form that is real within what the Islamic scholar Henri Corbin called the 'imaginal world', that is, the world that is pictured as being real by the worshipper. Nayler's devotion was not to the crucified Christ, but to the living Christ of the gospels, and so his identification took a different form. However, it was none-the-less real for that, and was as misunderstood by his fellow-religionists as some of the stigmatics have been.

Most of James Nayler's writings are deeply Christocentric, which is not surprising considering his attitude to and identification with God in the form of Jesus Christ. In his often quoted last words, written shortly before his death, he shows the depth of his mystical attainment.

> There is a Spirit which I feel that delights to do no evil, nor to revenge any wrong, but delights to endure all things, in hope to enjoy its own in the end. Its hope is to outlive all wrath and contention, and to weary out all exaltation and cruelty, or whatever is a nature contrary to itself. (QFP 19:12)

Remember, this passage was written just before Nayler died, and after he had been through the most horrendous persecution for nothing more than an ecstatic vision of his unity with Christ. Even Quakers had disowned him for a time, not understanding what had been going on, yet such was the power of this Loving Spirit that he had no emnity against them, and, following the example of Jesus, did not even die cursing those who had tortured and imprisoned him. This is one of the most beautiful affirmations of universal peace in the English language, and it came from one who, on the surface, was least likely to be aware of that Peace.

For Friends today, the understanding of the principles of ecstatic religion which can be gained from the study of other faiths, can help us to understand and appreciate the greatness of this outstanding early Friend. We may wonder what influence he might have had on Quakerism as a whole if Friends had fully understood the depth of his mystical experience, and the way in which it was expressed.

Quakers and Religious Language

The language used by early Friends in encouraging each other to go into the silence and there discover the Truth, is often not that of orthodox Christianity. In 1657, George Fox wrote to Friends, encouraging them to meet together and to "...know one another in that which is eternal, which was before the world was". Friends repeatedly use mystical and poetic language in encouraging the practice of meeting for worship. It must have seemed to them that, even though there is much poetry within the King James Bible, there was an inner urge to find a greater variation of language in order to fully express the wonder and the power that they were discovering in the simplicity of their new way of worshipping.

One final example shows the range of the vision and language of early Friends, even under extreme circumstances. The day before he was martyred in 1661, William Leddra of Barbados wrote these deeply inspiring words, which use the wonders of the natural world to describe his mystical experience.

As the flowing of the ocean doth fill every creek and branch thereof, and then retires again towards its own being and fullness, and leaves a savour behind it; so doth the life and virtue of God flow into every one of your hearts, whom he hath made partakers of his divine nature; and when it withdraws but a little, it leaves a sweet savour behind it; that many can say they are made clean through the word that he hath spoken to them. In which innocent condition you may see what you are in the presence of God and what you are without him... Stand still, and cease from thine own working, and in due time thou shalt enter into the rest, and thy eyes shall behold his salvation, whose testimonies are sure, and righteous altogether. (QFP 2:19)

Such language would be acceptable to adherents of many other faiths, and illustrates the variety of Quaker mystical experience. Its timing is again significant, showing that the spirit which was guiding and underpinning Quakerism was truly the Spirit of Peace.

I am not arguing that writing such as this means that all early Friends were, to use a contemporary term, 'Universalists'. Rather, I am trying to show that the experiences that they had, though firmly Christian, brought about the use of a language greater and more inclusive than could be found within the Christian theological tradition. They did this in order to show the reality of the Divine as found within the individual – regardless of belief. Their Christian experience did not bind them to orthodox Christian language, but was strong and deep enough for them to leave behind the limitations of words which might stifle the free expression of their experience. They were clear that God revealed Himself to any who were content to wait in silence for His word, and that such revelation came to ordinary folk as well as to the educated and the ordained.

This would be the basis of Quaker faith and practice for the next three hundred years and more. It is this which has led Friends to have an attitude to other faiths, philosophies and practices which, while remaining true to their own revelation, includes an openness to learn other ways of finding and expressing that same truth. While it would not be right to claim that this openness was unique to Friends, it was the basis on which today's Society was built.

Such an attitude has not been universally popular. Unprogrammed Quakers with a more Christocentric stance, to say nothing of Evangelical Friends from the programmed traditions in various parts of the world, do not share it. For them, it is Jesus Christ alone who is the aspect of God who is to be worshipped and revered, and we can only come to know God and His will through the teachings in the Bible. The open position of liberal Friends has led to some difficulties within the ecumenical movement, with some fundamentalist Christians denouncing Quakers as being a cult, with all the pejorative meanings that such a term implies.

All this poses a problem for Friends involved in the ecumenical and interfaith fields. It has been noted that it is often easier for people with radically differing backgrounds and practices to come to an understanding, while those who have a common heritage find it much more difficult. This was highlighted in the 'Quaker Conflicts' in the USA, between Friends of differing theological views. It eventually caused a number of 'splits', which resulted in the many and varied approaches to Quakerism that are found there today.[17]

I remember when I first attended a gathering of Friends in the USA. It was one of the early annual meetings of Quakers Uniting in Publications, an international group concerned with all aspects of Quaker publishing, bookselling and writing, which had representation from all shades of Quaker theology. I was the only representative from outside the USA, and I was asked about the situation in the UK. I replied that any fairly large meeting would have the same spread of theological opinion as was present at that meeting. Surprised by this answer, they asked, "How do you cope?" I had not thought much about it before, but it suddenly came to me that the key lay in our silent meeting for worship, where Friends try, for one hour, to leave concepts, differences and ideas outside the meeting room and to seek God's harmony together, regardless of what that might mean to each one present.

This idea of seeking harmony in the Silence is also the key to the Quaker approach to interfaith dialogue today. Loosely based on the concept of "Mutual Irradiation" pioneered by Douglas Steere, it was the inspiration to Margot Tennyson and myself when we founded the Friends Interfaith Group, and has been used in one form or another in much of Quaker work in this field.

CHAPTER 3

Mutual Irradiation

IN RECENT TIMES, Quaker involvement with other faiths has been based on three things. Firstly, there is the Quaker involvement with India, and secondly, the work of Mutual Irradiation pioneered by Douglas Steere. Out of these two have come a variety of other work, as, inspired by them, individual Friends have felt concerns. The third factor is the increased accessibility of the writings and teachings of other faith traditions, and the acceptance by Friends of the possibility of using these spiritual languages to express the experience of the Quaker Life.

Sri Ramakrishna

The story of modern Friends' involvement in interfaith work as such begins in India in the second half of the nineteenth century. One of the earliest references, which must have had an impact on many other people outside Quaker circles, is mentioned in *The Gospel of Ramakrishna* by 'M'. Sri Ramakrishna, or, to give him his full title, Ramakrishna *Paramahamsa* – literally, 'the greatest Swan', a title of great respect – came to be accepted as a Divine Incarnation, and is known as one of the great teachers of religious unity. He was poorly educated, but had from his earliest years a great desire to know God, and eventually achieved the vision of God as the Divine Mother. He soon became recognised as an enlightened soul. He practised many different disciplines, and affirmed from his personal experiences that, in addition to the various Hindu traditions, Christianity, Islam, Buddhism and all other faiths were valid pathways to the Divine.

The Gospel of Ramakrishna is a day-to-day account of a portion of his life written by one of his closest lay (non-monastic) disciples, Mahendranath Gupta, who writes under the pseudonym of 'M'. It is a beautiful account, sincerely recorded by someone who was present at the time, of the life and teachings of a truly great soul, a fact which shines through the pages of the book. Mahatma Gandhi, another great soul who will play a part in the Quaker interfaith story, said of the book, "The story of Ramakrishna Paramahamsa's life is a story of religion in practice. His life enables us to see God face to face".

25

In the entry for Saturday, October 31st 1885, M records.

It was about 11 o'clock in the morning. Sri Ramakrishna was sitting in his room with the devotees. He was talking to a Christian devotee named Misra. Misra was born in a Christian family in north-western India and belonged to the Quaker sect. He was thirty-five years old. Though clad in European fashion he wore the ochre cloth of a *sannyasi* under his foreign dress. Two of his brothers had died on the day fixed for the marriage of one of them, and on that very day Misra had renounced the world.

Misra: "It is Rama alone who dwells in all beings."

Sri Ramakrishna replied... "Rama is one but he has a thousand names. He who is called 'God' by the Christians is addressed by the Hindus as Rama, Krishna, Ishvara and other names. A lake has many *ghats*. The Hindus drink water at one *ghat* and call it '*Jal*', the Christians at another and call it 'water' and the Muslims at another and call it '*pani*'. Likewise, He who is God to the Christians is Allah to the Muslims."

Misra: "Jesus is not the son of Mary. He is God Himself. Now he (*pointing to Sri Ramakrishna*) appears as you see him – again, he is God Himself. You are not able to recognise him. I have seen him before in visions, though I see him now directly with my eyes."

Ramakrishna then went into *samadhi*, and, taking Misra by the hands, told him, "You will get what you are seeking."[(18)]

Other Movements of the Spirit in India

There were many other contacts between individuals and small groups of Friends in which they managed to come together in a unique way. The books, *Friends and other Faiths* by Margot Tennyson and *Quakers in India* by Marjorie Sykes tell of a number of these meetings. One of the most interesting concerns a group which came together in Calcutta after reading a copy of Barclays' *Apology*. This group was comprised of Christians, Hindus and Muslims, and could have been the group that Misra was associated with. They continued worshipping together unknown to the rest of the Quaker world for some fifteen years, and might have remained so, except that two of their members decided to journey to London for the Yearly Meeting in 1861. They obviously expected a warm and enthusiastic reception, but Margot Tennyson records that London Yearly Meeting "...was not quite as welcoming as it might have been".

The idea of the Spirit bringing together a group of people to wait in silence is not new, and I am certain that there are many such groups of which we have never heard, partly because it is a part of their tradition to remain hidden and work quietly. Abdu'l Baha of the Baha'i faith told Friends at Westminster Meeting of one such group called 'Followers of the Inner Light' that was founded in Persia about a thousand years ago, and was still in existence in 1913. Many Sufi groups relied similarly on silent waiting and inner guidance, while there were – and are – others in various mystery schools of the Hindu, Buddhist, Jewish, Christian, Muslim, and Taoist traditions. Some of these lived a monastic or other forms of communal life, while others made it a part of their tradition to be 'In the world but not of it', earning their living as craftsmen or in service to suffering humanity, while maintaining a hidden practice of 'prayer without ceasing'.

Geoffrey Maw, a Friend who was a Quaker missionary at Itarsi, made several trips into the Himalayas with Hindu pilgrims in order to share their spiritual experiences. He was accompanied by an Indian Friend, Khushilal. These journeys are recorded in the book, *Pilgrims in Hindu Holy Land*, which consists of his journal, edited by his daughter. Geoffrey Maw did not go as a missionary, nor as a tourist, but dressed in the ochre robe of a *sadhu*. In his introduction, he says:

> Why did I go? I am a foreigner and a Christian, and much of my active life has been spent working for the Society of Friends (Quakers) in the Hoshangabad District of the Central Provinces [of India]. There I tried to understand the aspirations and achievements of the Hindu religious life; I focused my interest on the pilgrims, and especially the *sadhus* who congregate at the holy places and along the sacred ways. I found that if I were to understand them I must know for myself something of the life of the pilgrim way. During some of my hot-weather holidays I have therefore gone on pilgrimage, and among my travels I have included this most famous pilgrimage of all.

Although dressed in the garb of a *sanyasin* (monk), he wore a wooden cross around his neck so that people would know that he was a Christian. He found little or no hostility to the fact that he was – or appeared to be – a Christian sanyasin – and became aware that many Hindu holy men were ready to recognise Jesus as an incarnation of God. In more recent times, Swami Abhishektananda and Father Bede Griffiths, both of whom were Catholic priests, were to find that the same openness, provided there were no efforts to convert people from Hinduism to Christianity. A friend of mine, a priest of the Liberal Catholic Church in India, told me that over two thirds of his congregation were Hindus, but they supported his church because he made no effort to make converts, and because he allowed and even encouraged all the congregation to receive holy communion.

Fellowship of Friends of Truth

Indian spiritual teachers and leaders in the social and political fields also accepted Friends and were willing to work with them. Mahatma Gandhi and Rabindranath Tagore were among those who had close links with Quakers, particularly respecting their oneness and the testimony to Peace and reconciliation.

Probably the first active involvement of Quakers in a venture that was truly interfaith in its conception came about in India in 1949, just after the tragic communal riots in Calcutta and Delhi which followed Indian independence. Horace Alexander, a Quaker who was working with Gandhi at the time, asked what Quakers might do to help the situation and re-establish trust between Hindus, Muslims and Sikhs. This led to the founding of what became known as The Fellowship of Friends of Truth.

Horace Alexander suggested to Gandhi that what was needed was a religious fellowship which could be joined by all adherents of the world's religions. This would not be a syncretist movement, but "a union of hearts"; a place in which people of each faith "...could find themselves at one, because they are seeking together to practise the truth of God in the world". He asked Gandhi whether the Quakers were the best people to help this process, or whether it would be better served by an Indian group such as the Brahmo Samaj or the Ramakrishna Mission. If that were the case, he would be willing to consider joining such a group. "No", Gandhi replied, "of the societies that I know, I do not think that any would be better or even so good. I think the Friends are the best. But only on one condition: are they prepared to recognise that it is as natural for a Hindu to grow into a Friend as it is for a Christian to grow into one" In his original statement, from which this is quoted, Horace Alexander comments that he particularly remembered the words "Grow into...". He says that he responded to Gandhi by saying, "Some would agree to this condition and some would not. I am one of those who would readily agree to that position, not only for Hindus but for Muslims and others". This would still seem to be the position within the Society of Friends.

Horace Alexander's original statement said:

Some of our Indian Friends, Hindu, Muslim, Sikh, Parsi as well as Christian, have worked with us, and we with them, in common enterprises for the relief of suffering; and we have joined together in acts of worship. Out of such deep friendship has grown a desire, sometimes expressed as a definite request, that some organic fellowship might be formed. So now we propose to try a new experiment: to invite any who care to do so to join a fellowship of truth. This will be open alike to members of the Society of Friends and to non-members, to Christians and non-Christians; to all without any test or condition of membership beyond a serious desire to associate themselves with the basis and goal of the Fellowship.

Horace Alexander brought this concern to Meeting for Sufferings to try to get the approval of the Society of Friends as a whole, but his concern was not accepted. The minute said in part:

> The new Fellowship springs from association with Gandhi, and owes much to his belief in the power of Truth to draw men into unity. It cannot in our view become the future expression of Quakerism in India.

Friends at this time were too far removed from what was going on in India, and also wished to maintain the approval of the other Christian Churches, which were committed to missionary activity to convert non-Christians. It would be some years before the Society of Friends was able once again to look at other faiths with the same openness as early Quakers such as William Penn.

Fortunately, India has a deep spiritual tradition of its own, and Horace Alexander received enough support there to go ahead and form the Fellowship. Although India has known examples of interfaith rivalry and even warfare, there have also been many examples of co-operation and understanding. Thus, many small groups continued to have a greater or lesser Quaker influence in their make-up, and an awareness of the Spirit of Unity that transcended religious barriers. The interaction of Quakerism with the Indian traditions would bear much fruit, and the Fellowship of Friends of Truth was a good example of what could be achieved. In 1961, it had 13 groups in India, and one in England, working quietly towards its ends. The greater results of this work were to come later, when those who were inspired by it followed their own concerns, and found that they were able to draw on the co-operation of a growing number of Friends.

The FFT was founded in November 1949, and its principle aim was to encourage adherents of the various faiths to worship God together. Each should continue to be true to his or her own faith, but none should despise another. The Fellowship was founded on three main points.

1) Reverence for all religions.
2) Silent worship
3) United brotherly action on non-violent lines.

It invited people of all faiths to share the richness of their traditions and to support each other in working for world peace and social justice.[19]

Mutual Irradiation

The next major concern which had an impact on later interfaith work within Friends was that of the American Quaker, Douglas Steere. He was a professor of philosophy at Haverford College in Philadelphia, and was the chairman of the Friends World Committee for Consultation for six years. He had a concern which grew slowly in the Quaker manner, and which was tested on a number of occasions between 1961 and 1965. He proposed that FWCC should arrange "two high-level unhurried conferences", one with Christians and Zen Buddhists in Japan, and the other in India between Christians and Hindus. Friends would be the catalysts for both of these gatherings, in which the emphasis would be on silent worship in the Quaker manner, and on speaking out of the silence in a way similar to worship sharing.

In the past, most interfaith work had been based on one of three approaches. Either one of the parties was trying to 'convert' the other, or they were trying to arrive at a form of syncretism. The third way is where each religion so honours the other that it makes no attempt to challenge it. Mutual Irradiation is a "fourth way", in which the atmosphere is provided where each faith may give the truest witness based on its deepest experiences. It enables each participant to be open, honest and true to themselves, while accepting the same from everyone else. It is a very subtle way of overcoming the difficulties presented by such gatherings, and it really has to be experienced in order to be fully appreciated and understood. In his Pendle Hill Pamphlet, *Mutual Irradiation*, Douglas Steere says:

> The fact of mutual irradiation is an existential one that goes beyond mere description and has to be experienced in order to be penetrated. It is not likely to leave any of the participants where they were when they started. But it may give a clue to the deeper dimension of what is meant by a truly ecumenical situation between the world religions.

In fact, any study based on this principle is a living example of the Spirit at work. If the group becomes fully gathered, then it becomes an example of what George Fox meant when he spoke of "the Power of the Lord" being "over all". Through this action, problems are accepted and overcome in a way that would be impossible even to the most detailed of human planning. And this is what happens. In the deep silence of the Spirit, the participants do not merely discuss, and certainly do not argue. The problems are faced fairly and squarely, and not neglected as happens sometimes in interfaith dialogue, and there is an interpenetration in which harmony and understanding arises in spite of the problems. Often Christians put viewpoints from a Buddhist or Hindu perspective, sometimes even without consciously meaning to do so.

It will be clear by now that Mutual Irradiation is more than just another talking shop. In fact, it is so important that I feel that it has been the basis – whether recognised, named or not – for most of Friends interfaith work in the twentieth century, and its possibilities have by no means been exhausted. It is what Douglas Steere calls "functional ecumenism". The core meaning of ecumenism is to embrace the world, and in a wonderfully eloquent, descriptive and poetic passage in his pamphlet *Mutual Irradiation* he elaborates on this theme.

A truly functional ecumenism wants to witness to the world how much God cares, and if this means stopping a war; or trying to learn how to share more equitably the world's material resources; or meeting an emergency human need or joining the poor; or sending brotherly teachers and companions to live and share with those in another area; or teaching one another how to meditate, or how to pray, or how to kindle corporate adoration, or how to grow in the life of devotion, or how to use the lives of past saints and heroes to re-kindle our commitment; or how great art, painting, sculpture and music can expand the soul; or how personal guidance and therapy may release the deeper life in us; or how the world of plants and animals and water and wind can temper our souls; a functional ecumenism will open us in these and other areas to the witness of our fellows, whether Christian or the adherents of other world religions.

This approach takes for granted that such irradiation is the interplay between equals, though each may have their own strengths and weaknesses. Functional ecumenism encourages each "...to practice our own religious tradition to the hilt and to share our experiences with each other in every creative way we can devise." There is no danger that any participant will be encouraged to leave their own faith for another.

It also assumes as its ground rule that we shall not seek to detach each other's members to swell our own numbers, though occasional transfers may take place. These need not be regarded as ecumenical casualties but rather be generously accepted on both sides.[20]

In a couple of recent books [*Spiritual advice for Buddhists and Christians* and *The Good Heart*] His Holiness the Dalai Lama has pointed out the close links that have emerged between Christian and Buddhist monks. He also encourages a process of exchange that is very similar to Mutual Irradiation, the deep practice of each faith, but strongly discourages people from changing their religion. He is also at pains to point out that the virtues of each religion – and types of practice within each religion – relate to the psychological types of people. A similar approach is found with the Hindu faith, where the different types of *bhakti* (devotion) *jnana* (reason) and *karma* (selfless action) require different practices, while acknowledging that each leads to the same Goal.

The Muslim poet-saint Jalaluddin Rumi had Christian, Jewish and animist disciples, and he encouraged each in their own way. One of his best loved poems speaks to us all, saying:

Come, come, whoever you are
Worshipper, wanderer, lover of learning;
Ours is not a caravan of despair
Even if you have broken your vows a thousand times
Come! come.[21]

31

The great saint of modern India, Sri Ramana Maharshi, likewise had disciples of different religions, and strongly discouraged their changing, saying, "You will only be changing the thought, 'I am a Hindu', for the thought, 'I am a Christian'", he told those who wished to change. He also said that there are two ways; know the Self or surrender the self. ('Self' with a capital equates with what Quakers call "That of God in everyone".)

The 'Colloquia'

The practical expressions of mutual irradiation came in the form of 'The Zen-Christian Colloquia' in Japan, and a similar gathering of Hindus and Christians in India. On both of these occasions Friends took the initiative in inviting the participants and organising the meetings, though the Christians were chosen to be ecumenically representative. They all lived together for up to a week and, although many of the participants were academics, no advance papers were issued. Each person was encouraged to speak from the heart, and there was plenty of time for questions and discussion. There was also free time available, in which many personal friendships were made which bore later fruit. No efforts were made to impress other participants, and the discussion was often intensely personal and very frank.

The Colloquia in Japan continued each year, and some of the results were later published in *A Zen-Christian Pilgrimage – The Fruits of Ten Annual Colloquia in Japan 1967-1976*, compiled by Yukio Irie, a Japanese Quaker professor who had also been the chair at the first gathering. Though there have been other such collections since, the book was – and possibly still is – unique, in that it includes papers by many of those who later became famous in the field of Buddhist/Christian studies, including Heinrich Dumoulin, William Johnston and Masao Abe. Yukio Irie's paper is entitled *The Fountainhead of Religion*, in which he movingly describes his journey from Zen Buddhism to Quakerism, moved by his despair following his mother's death and the Second World War.

This event bore further fruit for British Quakers when, in 1981, the Friends Interfaith Group invited Yukio Irie to England to share some of his experiences, and to give a lecture at the Group's annual meeting at Yearly Meeting. This he did very movingly, never disparaging Zen Buddhism, but only pointing out that it had not proved adequate to bring him peace of mind following the war. He freely acknowledged that it *had* been the way to a similar peace for others. It was observing the lives of two American Quakers, Thomas and Eliza Foulke, that had led him to Quakerism. They lived truly Christian lives without ever preaching Christianity, and he felt that it was this Grace of God that was the power that changed his own life and led him to become a Friend.

All those Friends who had the privilege of being with him during his short stay felt the continuing influence of this power. His own awareness of the Presence of God was something that we could feel, and we noted the way in which he would seem to be listening to a guiding voice, even in the middle of a conversation. His talk was very moving, with good English, but it was his silence that spoke loudest to us, and we were all grateful for the experience. His tenderness towards those who followed the traditional Japanese Buddhist faith was very noticeable. But allied to this was a firm conviction that Jesus' way – and the Quaker interpretation of it – was the right one for him. He taught us many lessons about inter-faith work, and we were profoundly grateful for his visit.

CHAPTER 4

Other Approaches

The Seekers

ANOTHER QUAKER INITIATIVE among British Friends which has led to greater interfaith understanding is a group called The Seekers Association. It was founded in 1946 under the chairmanship of Howard Collier. It is still in existence, and still working in a quiet way towards its original aims. From its beginnings it has not been limited to Friends, but has been open to all who share Quaker ideals and outlook. Its aims are currently to be found in a statement which is printed on the back of its journal, *The Seeker*.

> The Seekers Association ... consists of members of the Society of Friends and others who share their outlook. It aims to encourage the personal and corporate search for truth in a spirit of free and reverent enquiry, a spirit devotionally strong as well as intellectually honest. It seeks to relate religion to the study and experience of modern life and to provide fellowship among its members.

I said that it is working quietly, and this is particularly true because of the special way in which it works. Most of its work is done though "Correspondence Interest Groups", the subjects of which vary from year to year. They have looked at subjects ranging from aspects of Biblical study to the scriptures of other faiths; from the psychology of Jung to that of Eastern traditions such as Vedanta, Buddhism and Taoism. They have also looked at various aspects of parapsychology and its relation to mystical and religious thought. Quaker testimonies such as simplicity, and various ethical issues have also been the subjects of these groups. This year (1999) the subjects are "The Gospel According to Thomas", "Truth and Integrity" and a Worship Group, which is listed as being "Not quite the usual interest group, more a meeting for Worship by post".[22]

The Association publishes a twice yearly journal, which contains wide-ranging articles and thought-provoking discussion on all the subjects mentioned above, and many more. They encourage members to write and share experiences and ideas, and welcome controversy as something that arises naturally out of varieties of experience. They also have an annual conference on a particular theme, and they also hold an open session at Britain Yearly Meeting.

Members of The Seekers have always sought to look outwards from a narrow Quaker viewpoint, while at the same time recognising that Friends have much to share with the world. They are also aware of the need for changing Quaker thinking to be in tune with the present age. As an association, they recognise the limited impact that they have had on Quaker thought, but still feel that they have something to say which may be helpful to the Society in the years ahead. As a sign of this, the Spring 1999 issue of their journal carries an editorial, "What is a Seeker", in which the history of the Seekers is considered, and the need to re-evaluate their work is accepted.

The Open Letter Movement (OLM)

The Friend of 28th November 1975 published an "Open Letter to Friends" signed by four friends, Richard Allen, Lorna Marsden, Gerald Richards and Peter Tennant, to which Friends were invited to respond. This was the foundation of what came to be called the Open Letter Movement. The original letter put a number of questions relating to the present state of Quaker faith, and among them was one which asked "How do we meet the insights into spiritual awareness now coming from the East?" Although the Open Letter Movement has not been specifically concerned with interfaith matters, this question attracted a number of Friends who were to become members. Interfaith matters are seen as a part of the whole question about the inner life of the Society of Friends today. The OLM holds conferences each year, and several of the early ones were held with the Friends Interfaith Group and the Quaker Universalist Group.

The aims of the OLM are broad, and include exploration of the discipline of waiting on the spirit at the still centre of our worship, stimulating new growth and fresh insights based on traditional Quaker witness, encouraging individual growth and providing a forum for the exchange of views. Such aims are creative in terms of interfaith dialogue within the Society of Friends.

The work of the OLM continues to develop. It is, in the best sense, a facilitation group bringing Friends together to consider problems in the traditional Quaker way, based on worship and inner listening. In recent years its conferences have not been specifically on inter-faith themes, but are always related to the underlying constants that are common to all religions. The OLM is unique among Quaker groups in that it does not have a formal committee structure. All its activities are co-ordinated by a small group or 'nucleus' who try to guide its activities based on its principles.[23]

The Quaker Universalist Group (QUG)

In the late 1970s there were two developments in the UK which led the work of Interfaith dialogue forward. These were the founding of the Quaker Universalist Group, and the Friends Interfaith Group, both in 1978. It was interesting that these two developments should have happened independently within the same year, and I believe that this is another example of the work of the Spirit in this field. What seems to happen is that a spiritual impulse is – for want of a better word – broadcast. This is received by some people sensitive to it, and it takes form as a concern, which may lead to the setting up of a group to take it forward in the Quaker manner.

In 1977, John Linton gave a lecture to the Seekers Association.[24] His main theme was that one did not have to be a Christian to be a Quaker. His lecture arose out of his experiences in India, where he was aware of similar movements of the Spirit to those mentioned previously, and was exposed to their influence. He also had taken part in worshipping groups where not only Quakers but other Christians, Hindus and Muslims had come together for silent worship after the manner of Friends, and found a harmony that clearly indicated to him that the professed faith of individuals was not a barrier. His lecture inspired a number of other Friends, and in 1978 a group was formed.

The QUG has grown over the years. It holds conferences, publishes an excellent journal and a number of pamphlets, and provides a forum through which matters relating to its aims can be discussed. Its current statement differs from the original one in a few small but significant ways.

> The Quaker Universalist Group is based on our understanding that spiritual awareness is accessible to everyone of any religion or none, and that no one person and no one faith can claim to have a final revelation or monopoly of Truth. We acknowledge that such awareness may be expressed in many different ways. We delight in this diversity and warmly welcome both Quakers and non-Quakers to join with us.[25]

The growth of the Quaker Universalist Group was not popular with all Friends. The fact that the Universalist viewpoint had become an organised part of the Quaker movement has led to some polarisation within Britain Yearly Meeting. This is usually seen as a division between Christocentric and Universalist Friends, but such a division is not really accurate. By its expressed aims, Universalism must include the Christian viewpoint, or it is not truly universal. However, in some of the early statements, it did appear that it was only Christian thought that was being criticised.

Taking forward the theme of John Linton's original talk, the Quaker Universalists developed the concern that it was not necessary to be a

Christian to be a Quaker. In the years since the formation of the QUG, most Monthly Meetings have accepted this principle, and allowed into membership seekers whose spiritual journey harmonised with Friends. This has meant that there are now Buddhist, Hindu, Humanist, Jewish, Muslim, and Pagan Quakers; though I feel that Christians of one kind or another are probably in the majority. This new openness to membership has not been without its critics, but generally there are enough shared values to make worship in the silence a meaningful experience to all concerned.

Among the criticisms of Quaker Universalism is that some have felt that it advocates a syncretic form of religion, an amalgamation which is neither one thing nor another. It seems to the critics that in this way it is losing much of the essential basis of each faith, and certainly the essential basis of Quakerism. Its critics feel that what is being sacrificed on the altar of unity is not only belief structures, the myths on which each religion is built, but also the spiritual disciplines that each faith gives to those who are interested enough to accept that faith as it actually is. In his Pendle Hill Pamphlet, *Letter to a Universalist*, John Punshon writes of the need for mutual respect and tolerance among different faiths, but not at the expense of watering down what they are to fit some external idea. He draws attention to the fact that he (and I know that this is true for many others) sometimes feels unable to minister at Meeting, because the words that he would naturally use are those of Christianity, with references to Jesus, salvation, and the Father God. There is also a difficulty in hearing too much 'universal' ministry. It is this sort of problem that could split meetings apart.

Universalists have heard these criticisms, and have on the whole listened sympathetically to them, while insisting that they have never advocated any particular form of religion, syncretic or otherwise. It seems that at the present time there is a growing understanding in the Universalist movement that Christianity has to be given its proper place among the spiritual 'Ways', and that for many Friends, the Society is a fundamentally – though not fundamentalist – Christian body. There seems to be a strong desire to reconcile any splits that may have taken place, and a very positive attitude towards those who hold different views. This has not decreased the Universalists own desire to be heard, and to be accepted for what they are within the corporate body of Friends. However, it has led to a general decrease in the polarisation, and has allowed greater freedom of discussion. Universalists hope that this will continue.

In 1994, three prominent Friends, Alastair Heron, Ralph Hetherington and Joseph Pickvance, coming from differing viewpoints within the Society, submitted a statement to Yearly Meeting. This was later included in *Quaker Faith and Practice* and has done much to help resolve the differences between Christocentric and Universalist Friends, and to show that this division is not based on spiritual reality. The statement read:

> We have acquired a much greater understanding of non-Christian religions from newcomers who have settled in this country since the end of World War II and this has increased the sympathy and respect of many Friends for these faiths. This broader approach to religion has led to an affirmation by 'Universalist' Friends that no one faith can claim to be a final revelation or to have a monopoly of the truth and to the rejection of any exclusive religious fundamentalism whether based on Christianity or any other religion.

The ferment of thought in this post-war period has produced a wide variety of beliefs in our Religious Society today and not a little misunderstanding on all sides. Intolerance has reared its head. Some Friends have voiced objections to the use of Christian language in meetings for worship and for business; others have been told that there is no place for them in our Religious Society if they cannot regard themselves as Christians. It has become quite customary to distinguish between 'Christians' and 'Universalists' as if one category excluded the other.

This situation has led many Friends to suppose that Universalist Friends are in some way set over against Christocentric Friends. This is certainly not the case. Universalism is by definition inclusivist, and its adherents accept the right to free expression of all points of view, Christocentric or any other. Indeed, in London Yearly Meeting [as it was at that time] there are many Universalists whose spiritual imagery and belief are thoroughly Christocentric.

From the beginning the Quaker Christian faith has had a universal dimension. George Fox saw the Light 'shine through all' and he identified it with the divine Light of Christ that 'enlightens every man that comes into the world' (John 1:9). He pointed out, as did William Penn in greater detail, that individuals who had lived before the Christian era or outside Christendom and had no knowledge of the Bible story, had responded to a divine principle within them. In these terms, all Quaker Christians are Universalists. Obedience to the Light within, however that may be described, is the real test of faithful living. (QFP 27:04)

Damaris and Frederick Parker-Rhodes

One other influence was very important for me personally, and without it, much of the work that I have managed to do with Friends could not have taken place. A major turning point in my Quaker life and thought came with the 1977 Swarthmore Lecture, *Truth, a Pathway not a Possession*, which was given by Damaris Parker-Rhodes. I had reached a point in my Quaker life when I had almost decided that the Society of Friends was not the right place for me. It seemed to me at that time that there was no-one who related to my interests in interfaith work and my studies in parapsychology and spiritual healing. I attended Damaris's lecture in a sad and resigned state of mind. In fact, I cannot fully remember why I attended it. But I am so glad that I did.

In a simple and straightforward way, Damaris spoke of her life story and her spiritual search. Her involvement in left-wing politics, and her discovery of the inner mystical side of her being left me in a state of wonderment. She said so many things that rang bells with me, and which I found so helpful. Most of all, I left with the feeling that here was someone who understood, and that I would be able to find a spiritual home within the Religious Society of Friends.

In the printed version of her lecture Damaris acknowledges her own debt to Douglas Steere, but expresses it in her own unique fashion, getting to the essence of the Quaker contribution to interfaith studies, which is to find the depths of our own tradition while listening to what others have to say.

> In a few years' time it may be as common for people here to be Buddhist, Hindu or New Age Meditators of various kinds, as to be Christian. Certainly in our present era of 'mutual irradiation' (the title of a Pendle Hill Pamphlet by Douglas Steere) both Eastern and western faith is likely to be enriched, but only if we seek inwardly to grasp what is most precious in our own tradition.

Later on in the book, she looks with the same penetrating insight into the ways in which other traditions can enrich our own, by making us more conscious of the hidden depths of our own. As someone who had joined the Society deeply committed to the Buddhist tradition, yet intuitively aware that Quakerism had much more to offer than I had yet explored, she confirmed my original feeling that I had been right to become a Quaker, a feeling that had been waning with the lack of understanding that I had been finding in my own and other meetings.

> A number of Friends both here and in America, are at the present time in this movement of search, practising Transcendental Meditation (TM), learning Yoga and T'ai Chi, Zen and Theravada Meditation and working with Sufis – and I count myself among them. This is not just shopping around, but is rather a serious experiment with truth which for me has made Quaker Christianity the more precious.

It was not just other traditional faiths that she was interested in. She was always concerned with the development of the individual and also of the community. New discoveries in psychology and the human development movement were also, for her, valid spiritual paths, though with some reservations.

Some brands of mysticism and meditation now currently claim to be seeking the development of human potential, while not believing in Christ, Buddha or Krishna. Where this quest is related to the search for wisdom and deeper truth about human values it is certainly a religious search... While that may be so, there is no doubt that any development of human potential has its possible misuse. Increased power must be increased power for either good or evil, for love and fellowship or for self interest. Everything depends on what the goal, or lack of goal, may be.

This perception of the goal is always related to the Quaker vision of 'That of God' in us all.

As a Friend I see this rising potential in Man as the Christ Within, the Seed and the Inward Light, and I believe that the pattern of the cross and resurrection shows its historical struggle to fulfilment as well as the path for each of us. Saints, geniuses of all kinds, prophetic visionaries, as well as all self-giving lovers, are part of the spiritual emergence.[26]

I did not make any effort to speak to Damaris after her lecture, but I felt moved to write her a long letter explaining my difficulties and how much I had appreciated her lecture. The almost immediate response was an invitation to come to visit her and Frederick at their home in Cambridge, something we soon arranged. Out of this grew a deep friendship from which I derived great inspiration, and which led to much of my future work with Friends.

The other significant aspect of visits to their Cambridge home was in meeting Frederick, Damaris's husband and partner in the spiritual search. Though his journey took him along different pathways – he was a pure mathematician and a great expert on fungi – yet they complemented and supported each other in a great number of ways. From Frederick I learned about listening. It was quite usual for Damaris, Beryl and I to be discussing some deep ethical or spiritual subject while Frederick seemed to be dozing by the fire. After we had gone around the subject – often seemingly for hours – Frederick would open his eyes and say a few words that not only summed up what we had been saying, but also added to it in a significant way.[27]

Sadly, I think, Damaris's Swarthmore Lecture was never reprinted, otherwise it might have had a greater impact on the interfaith work of Friends. However, she did write another book, *The Way Out is the Way In*, which incorporated some of the lecture material, and which told more of her personal journey, including her later struggle with cancer, which brought her back to a renewed appreciation of Christianity. Right at the end of this book, she sums up her discoveries of the Quaker way, and her prophetic vision for its future.

Quakers are bridge people. I remain on that bridge, part of my roots reaching back into the Christian past, and part stretching forward into the future where new symbols are being born.

The Friends Interfaith Group

I have first-hand knowledge about the Friends Interfaith Group, because I was directly involved in its founding. However, it would never have happened if it had not been for the vision of another prophetic woman Friend, Margot Tennyson. Margot had a deep and abiding basic concern; that contemporary Quakers need not just be Christians, and need not use solely Christian language to express their beliefs, experiences and practices. It would not be too much to say that she devoted her life to this concern, which manifested in various forms and projects over the years. One of these was the Friends Interfaith Group.

Its roots can be found in the *East Comes West Exhibition Project* which Margot Tennyson had begun in 1969 as part of the Gandhi Centenary celebrations. The original exhibition was called *The Arts of Village India*, and began life as an exhibition to help teachers gain some insight into the lives and beliefs of their growing number of Asian pupils. At the same time, the Gandhi Peace Foundation had contacted the Quaker's Asia Committee – of which Margot was a member – to see if it could help with fostering understanding between Hindus, Muslims and Sikhs in the UK. This inspired Margot to include sections about Asian religions in the exhibition. It proved very successful, and eventually 25 exhibitions were staged throughout England, and one in Scotland, at which there were opportunities for members of the three faiths to get together and meet, often for the first time.

Friends asked Margot to bring the exhibition to Yearly Meeting at York, and she agreed to bring the religious part, and to add sections on Buddhism and Judaism. In conjunction with this, it was agreed that there should be a meditation group, and to the surprise of all concerned, 135 Friends took part. Most of them admitted that they had been influenced by a spiritual teacher from another tradition, and, while not wishing to leave Quakers, were overjoyed to be able to share their experiences with other sympathetic Friends, many having thought that they were alone in their interests.

While the exhibition was being staged, Margot worked one day a week in the Quaker Community Relations Committee office in Friends House,

London, and it was here that I met her. I had been interested in interfaith matters for many years, having first come to Friends from being a member of a Buddhist group, and from the study and practice of Yoga. I had also been Assistant Manager at Watkins Bookshop in the West End of London for several years. Watkins was the major specialist bookshop dealing with all aspects of mysticism and comparative religion, and was a magnet for many people who were involved in this field.

Margot had had her own involvement with other faiths all through her life. Born of Jewish parents in Germany in 1921, she went through the early part of the Nazi persecution including the appalling Crystal Night. Following this, she was sent to London for her own safety, and it was here that she first encountered Quakers, who were very kind and supportive to her. It was perhaps natural that she should eventually become a member, but she told me on a number of occasions that she could never feel herself to be a Christian. The greatest early influence on her life was Gandhi, who made an almost mystical impression on her from her early teens. In her autobiography, *The Inner and Outer Become One*, she describes it.

> I have never been able to find out why Gandhi had such an enormous influence on my life right from my early teens. I can't recall even how I heard of him for the first time....I recall a night when I was standing under a very clear sky covered with stars and I felt an intuitive awareness of being part of a bigger scheme. I knew then with certainty that the happenings of Nazi Germany were totally unacceptable and evil; but I knew clearly that I could never employ violence to overcome it....Gandhi's non-violent resistance became the answer for me. I was sure then as I am now that soul-force was the weapon that was bound to bring success in the end, however long it might take.

Her contact with Quakers led her to India, and eventually to spend time with Gandhi at *Sevagram*, which was one of the greatest moments of her life. India also had another influence on Margot, which led her to study Vedanta, and eventually to the Ramakrishna Centre in London, where she met her teacher, Swami Bhavyananda. The Swami was also very involved with interfaith work, and so it was natural that Margot should be attracted to the Centre, where she learned to meditate. Vedanta teaches the harmony of all religions, and this particular movement was founded by Sri Ramakrishna, who has been mentioned earlier, and by his chief disciple Swami Vivekananda.

Margot and I found that we had much in common, having both been involved in different aspects of interfaith work for some time, and with many mutual friends in those circles. We both felt a deep concern that Friends needed to be more involved in interfaith matters, and felt that

42

they had much to contribute, as well as having much to learn. Quaker Meeting Houses throughout the country were being used by groups from other faiths, as well as for interfaith gatherings. We met together on many occasions before becoming convinced that we had a genuine concern in the area, and the Friends Interfaith Group was slowly born.

From the beginning, we felt moved to base the group on the principles of Douglas Steere's *Mutual Irradiation*, which we felt could add a new dimension to the work that had not been fully explored. We drew up a statement which read:

> We have formed a small group of adherents of different faiths to explore a union of hearts, where they may find themselves at one, because they are seeking the Truth together in silence and meditation. We do not aim at some syncretic experience of the different approaches to the World Faiths, but rather to experience and share in humility the unity that lies beyond the diversity in our beliefs. We are an informal group of Friends and others who want to explore the silence with members of different faiths as a unique and positive Quaker contribution to the interfaith dialogue which is going on around us.[28]

We also felt that the emphasis should be on the informality of the group, and the fact that it was a concern. We did not feel that we wanted any organisation, so we rejected the committee structure, and all forms of membership. We did not have a clerk, secretary, chair or other officers. Margot and I started with those friends that we had within the various faith communities, and we received considerable support. At first we were supported by the Quaker Community Relations Committee and its then Secretary, Albrecht Turk, and any donations that came in were passed to that committee. Later, as the emphasis of that Committee changed, we became self-supporting, but we never formally appealed for funds, and found that there were just enough donations from Friends who were equally concerned for us to carry out the work. Meetings tended to be self-supporting, with hardly ever anything left over, and we were grateful that – being a Quaker concern – we were not charged for rooms when we met at Friends House and elsewhere.

For some time, the mainstay of our work consisted in monthly meetings at Friends House, where we had an invited speaker who would share with us something of the depth of his tradition. The meeting began and ended in silence, and the speaker would speak from that silence when he or she was ready. There was time for questions and discussion, before the meeting ended with more silent reflection. We were usually able to make tea at the end of the meeting, and people would bring a little light food, sweets or biscuits to share. Though there was an atmosphere of harmony, we did not hesitate to bring up matters that could be controversial, though they were dealt with in a spirit of acceptance. Many new friendships were made, and new understandings reached. Among the subjects that we dealt with, in addition to the main Faith traditions, were Sufism, Yoga, Humanism and Spiritualism.

There was some controversy about this last subject, as some felt that we were getting involved in occult matters. The speaker, Bill Harrison, a minister from a South London Spiritualist church, managed to convince the mixed group representing seven different faiths that Spiritualism was a religion in its own right, to which the worship of God and service to our neighbours was as important as the proving of survival of bodily death. He also emphasised the work of spiritual healing which was one of the main activities in his church, linking it with the work of the Friends Fellowship of Healing.

The group invited teachers from other traditions such as Swami Bhavyananda and Ven. Vajiragnana, a senior monk from the Theravadin Buddhist Sangha, to lead one day retreats for Friends, and to teach us meditation. These days were usually held at William Penn House in London. We also organised visits to various centres, such as the London Mosque and a Sikh Gudwara, where we were warmly welcomed and allowed to share in the life of the community. These one-day retreats led to Interfaith Weekends, based on the principles of mutual irradiation, which were held at Charney Manor and at Woodbrooke College in Birmingham, and which were very successful.

Our remaining activity was to organise events at Yearly Meeting. This we did for a number of years. The events included an annual talk and worship sharing groups, all of which were well attended. Among the speakers we had were Swami Tripurananda, the English Vedantin monk who is also a Quaker, the Zen Buddhist writer Anne Bancroft who had been brought up among Quakers, and Rabbi Jeffrey Newman, Rabbi of the Finchley Reform Synagogue. These three talks were published in a booklet called *Three Spiritual Journeys*, now sadly out of print. Other speakers were Yukio Irie, the Japanese Quaker professor referred to earlier, and Ajahn Sumedho, a Western Theravadin monk who was at that time the abbot of Chithurst Buddhist Monastery in Sussex.

The Friends Interfaith Group continued to exist until 1988, though in its later years not very actively. In 1988, the Committee for Christian Relationships was asked by Meeting for Sufferings to set up a Sub-committee on Other Faiths, and to officially take over the responsibility for the Society's involvement in interfaith matters. Before it was finally laid down, the Group did two last things. It published a little booklet of quotations, both Quaker and from other traditions, and this is reproduced in this book as Appendix 1.

We also called one final meeting, to which we invited all the friends who had helped us through the years, together with members of the Committee for Christian Relationships. The purpose of this meeting was to ask the other-faith representatives what Friends could do for them in an official way. Several interesting points emerged. One was emphasis on the value of the Quaker meeting house as a place where people could meet without the distraction of religious symbols, and where the atmosphere was welcoming and supportive. Another thing was that Friends were seen as good mediators, who did not take sides, and our services would be welcomed when there was any trace of inter-religious conflict.

Quaker Committee for Christian and Interfaith Relationships (CIR)

Interfaith matters were at long last being taken seriously by the Society as a whole. This was something that Margot and I had long dreamed of, a dream shared by other members of the FIFG. Though we had sought this for some time, many of us had grave doubts as to whether the Committee for Christian Relationships was the right place for this to happen. However, Meeting for Sufferings decided that it would not be right to set up a new body for this purpose, so it was agreed that those working in the field would be asked to support the Committee in its work.

CIR (as it has become known) has had a great deal of work relating to Quaker membership of Churches Together in England, and this has meant that it has been proceeding rather slowly with its interfaith work. Up until the present time, most of its interfaith work has been concerned with surveying the work already done, and in relating to the interfaith activities of other church and ecumenical bodies. It has produced a number of reports and organised several conferences and its other main contribution has been to explore whether there can be a specifically Quaker theology in relation to other faiths. In this work the Committee has had the help of a number of Friends already involved in the field of Quaker theology. However, it does not, as far as I know, seem to have taken on board the distinctive Quaker work inspired by Douglas Steere, which the Interfaith Group had pioneered.

Only time will tell whether the placing of official Quaker interfaith work within this Committee has been a right move, or whether it needed a separate approach from that of Christian ecumenical relations. It is difficult for a large committee such as CIR, with a heavy workload covering many areas, to act with the same freedom and inspiration as a small informal group which has only to be accountable to itself. It may be that the interfaith work pioneered by the FIFG will be carried on by the Universalists, the Seekers, the Open Letter Movement or even some independent Friends. It is certainly to be hoped that the experiential approach to interfaith sharing which Quakers have pioneered will not be lost.

CHAPTER 5

Meditation and the Meeting
for Worship

The Big Question

IN ALL THE YEARS that I have been working with Friends in the field of interfaith matters I have been asked many questions. The most usual ones, and some of the more unusual ones, form the substance of this book. However, there is one question which stands out above all the others, both in the number of times I have been asked it, in the degree to which the answer matters to the questioner, and in the complexity of the answer. It is, on the face of it, a very simple question, which takes a number of forms. I will list the most usual ones, but basically it is all the same question, though the emphasis is different. It is this difference in emphasis that makes the question unique to each questioner. The most usual forms are:

- Is the meeting for worship the same as meditation?
- Is meditation the same as meeting for worship?
- Is the meeting for worship a form of meditation?

In looking for the answer, I will try to view the question as a whole, as well as looking at its constituent parts. When I say "the answer", I am aware that there is not really one answer. There are many shades of meaning to be explored, as well as many possibilities for individuals. I have done considerable research on approaches to meditation in the various world faiths, and I have found that they fall into two categories. These are recognised in, for example, the Hindu tradition, as *bhakti* (devotion) and *jnani* (knowledge), and in Japanese Buddhism as *tariki* (other power) and *jiriki* (self power).

Some meditation practices seem to be more or less identical to what we mean by meeting for worship, namely, waiting in silence (either in a group or alone) so that God's grace may bring a unity and a deep awareness of the Divine Presence. The gains which come through these practices are recognised as being gifts from God. Then there are the other kind of meditation practices in which the meditator does all the work, and gains the benefits, mostly as a solitary endeavour. There are also many which are a combination of both. From each type of experience comes not only inspiration and power to live our daily lives in a right way, but the possibilities of helping the suffering world.

In view of the importance of this question as seen by Friends who are becoming involved with other faith traditions, it is surprising how little has been written on the subject, particularly in the UK. There are two works written by American Quakers which have given me help and inspiration in investigating this difficult subject. I am most grateful to them. They are the Pendle Hill Pamphlet called *Quaker Worship and Techniques of Meditation* by Scott Crom, and the book *Meditation the Inward Art* by Bradford Smith. Both have been available in this country (though now sadly out of print), but it is interesting to observe that the latter is almost unknown among Friends, while the former went out of print very quickly, in spite of the fact that there was a big demand for it. I do not necessarily agree with everything that they have to say on the subject, nor even with all their conclusions, but any study of this subject needs to start by acknowledging a debt to these writings.

I hate to have to say this, but the real answer to the overall question must begin with the well-known, much loved and often abused get-out: "It all depends on what you mean by...". Unfortunately this is true. We cannot begin to look at this profound subject, which has implications for much of the work that Friends have done with people of other faiths, without some definitions. We do have to know what we are talking about when we say "meditation" and "meeting for worship".

Meanings

The Dictionary definitions of 'meditation' and 'worship' are a helpful place to start. The *New Shorter Oxford English Dictionary* defines meditation as "The action or practice of profound spiritual or religious reflection or mental contemplation" which I think most Friends will agree can – though does not always – take place in meeting for worship, and would seem on the face of it to be a valid activity in meeting. Worship, with its root meaning of the "acknowledgement of worth" is seen in religious terms as "Religious reverence, adoration or homage paid to a being or power regarded or treated as supernatural or divine; the expression of this in acts, ritual, ceremony or prayer, especially of a public or formal nature." I wonder if Friends think of Meeting for Worship in these terms?

Another helpful place to start lies in the title of the Scott Crom's pamphlet. He refers not just to 'meditation' but to *techniques* of meditation'. (*my emphasis*). This is where the problem lies. When people talk about meditation, they often have a particular approach, such as Zen or

47

Transcendental Meditation in mind. They might be thinking of meditation as taught in the world-wide Christian Meditation Movement founded by Father John Main, or even the Jesus Prayer from the Orthodox tradition. They might be thinking of the Buddhist mindfulness of breathing as taught by the Vietnamese Buddhist master Thich Nhat Hanh, who has done so much work for peace, and has thus come in contact with Friends, or an aspect of meditation taught within the disciplines of Yoga. All these and many others come within the heading of "techniques", and I believe that it is these that many Friends find difficult to contemplate as having a place within our beloved Meeting for Worship.

Yet even here, they *can* have a place. Many of them help to still the mind, and so are useful in the process of centring down. If they are used for a short while – and provided they are not intrusive to other Friends in terms of external sounds, movements or postures – then they can be helpful, so long as the worshipper realises that the aim is to surrender to a simple waiting, and that ultimately the gathered meeting is a gift from God, rather than anything that we do for ourselves. As the *Advices and Queries* tell us, "We seek a gathered stillness in our meetings for worship so that all may feel the power of God's love drawing us together and leading us". (A & Q #8)

Worship

Our pure idea of the simplicity of meeting for worship tends to be idealistic. The idea of waiting on God may appear simple, but it is by no means easy. It takes practice. The moment we try to sit quietly and allow our minds to settle, it seems to be the perfect excuse for them to run riot with thoughts. The more we try to be silent, or to concentrate on matters relating to the spiritual life, the more the mind – 'the monkey mind' as Hindus call it – behaves just like a restless monkey swinging aimlessly from branch to branch. It is here that the use of techniques may be helpful for a while, so long as they are seen as a means and not an end.

John Edward Southall, a nineteenth century Quaker printer, has – for me – one of the clearest descriptions of the difficulties and joys of Quaker worship. He had his own technique, which was to keep turning the mind back to thoughts of God when he became aware of the monkey mind. He tells how he had read that God was waiting in the depths of his being to talk to him, if only he would get still enough to hear. He thought this would be very easy:

But I had no sooner commenced than a perfect pandemonium of voices reached my ears, a thousand clamouring notes from without and within, until I could hear nothing but their noise and din.... Then came the conflicts of thoughts for the morrow, but God said, 'Be Still'.

48

And as I listened, and slowly learned to obey, and shut my ears to every sound, I found, after a while, that when other voices ceased, or I ceased to hear them, there was a still small voice in the depths of my being that began to speak with an inexpressible tenderness, power and comfort.'

In the meeting for worship we, like John Edward Southall, may start by trying to think thoughts of God, in order to provide a space where we can listen to the 'still small voice' through which God within us speaks. We may have to bring our minds back to the subject time after time. This bringing back the mind may be helped by awareness of our breathing, or by the use of a mantra or what is called a centring prayer, a short word or phrase that reminds us of God. This can be dropped as the strong feeling of oneness with God and with each one present develops, and the meeting is 'gathered'. As this happens, we no longer need techniques. The distracting thought-voices and the activity of the 'monkey mind' become still, in a way that we can neither anticipate nor achieve by our own efforts.

Robert Barclay's famous description of Meeting for Worship is well-known and often quoted, and has been the means of bringing a number of Friends to their first meeting.

When I came into the silent assemblies of God's people, I felt a secret power among them, which touched my heart, and as I gave way to it, I found the evil weakening in me and the good raised up. So I became thus knit and united unto them, hungering more and more after the increase of this power and life. ...'.[30]

Another Early Friend, Francis Howgill, spoke about the experience of the Divine Presence in meeting, and told how for him and others present,

'The Lord of heaven and earth we each found to be near at hand as we waited upon him in pure silence'.[31]

A more recent description, and one which contemporary Friends can more easily identify with, is given by Caroline Stephen, the aunt of the novelist Virginia Woolf.

One never-to-be-forgotten Sunday morning, I found myself one of a small company of silent worshippers who were content to sit together without words, that each one might feel after and draw near to the Divine Presence, unhindered at least, if not helped, by any human utterance. Utterance I knew was free, should the words be given; and before the meeting was over, a sentence or two were uttered with great simplicity by an old and apparently untaught man, rising in his place among the rest of us. I did not pay much attention to the words he spoke and I have no recollection of their purport. My whole soul was filled with the unutterable peace of the undisturbed opportunity for communion with God, with the sense that at last I have found a place where I might, without the faintest suspicion of insincerity, join with others in simply seeking His presence. To sit in silence could at least pledge me to nothing; it might open to me (as it did that morning) the very gate of heaven.[32]

No mention of techniques here. The silence is enough. It is the presence of God which performs the miracle of stilling the restless mind.

This 'gathering', the 'opening of Heaven's gate', and the resultant feeling of the reality of God's presence, is, and must always be, the heart of the worship. If techniques can help us achieve the receptive state of mind that is necessary to experience this and to share it with others, then we should not be afraid of them. But it is vital to acknowledge that they are not an end in themselves.

Meditation

In looking more closely at meditation, there are two definitions that I have found helpful regarding meditation in general, and particularly in relation to Quakers. One comes from Bradford Smith's book *Meditation the Inward Art*. I would like to quote from the introduction.

Meditation is good in and for itself because it is an active working of the whole personality – emotions, intellect, spirit. More, it draws the isolated individual into the universal and makes the connection so clear that no one who learns the art of meditation can ever feel alone or isolated in a hostile universe.

He goes on to ask, "What is meditation?", and answers, not with any description of techniques, but with the example of Thoreau, who so ordered his life that he had time for all things, great and small, and was able to discover the unity of nature and the universe while he sat alone in his cabin. Bradford Smith also quotes Emerson, who wrote; "The finished man is he who in the midst of the crowd keeps with perfect sweetness the independence of solitude".

Bradford Smith continues.

Meditation implies a concern with fundamental things, but does not limit or define them. One may come through meditation to a sense of the presence of God as a real and living person, a kind of super-father. Or the sense of presence may come as a merging with the world of nature until one feels caught up in its processes and becomes one with sunlight and wind and birdsong and clouds floating. Or a sense of well-being may flood into the consciousness and irradiate it with a conviction of the presence of goodness – the goodness of life, of experience, of friendship and childhood and love. Or the sense of unity with something beyond self may come as a sensation of light flooding inward – through closed eyelids into the quiet and receptive mind, into every cavern and nerve of the body. Or it may be simply a feeling of peace and contentment.

This description of meditation will, I feel also ring bells with Friends' experiences in Worship.

The other definition is shorter, more concise, and yet says all that needs to be said. It was given to me by an Indian teacher, Swami Chidananda of the Divine Life Society. It is: "Meditation is what happens when everything else ceases".[33] This could be a definition of the gathering of a Quaker meeting.

From these examples it will be clear that in looking at meditation in this way, we are considering something far more than dictionary definitions, or techniques designed to bring about a specific result. Viewed this way, meditation is seen, not as something esoteric and mysterious, but as a natural process. In fact, many of the worlds' greatest spiritual lights – from a variety of faith traditions – have described it as being the most natural thing in the world. When asked about it, one Zen master said it was "Nothing special", while another described it as being "The mind you were born with" through which you recognise birds singing or dogs barking when you hear them. An Indian teacher, Nisargadatta Maharaj, described it as "Your natural state" and Brother Mandus, of the Christian World Healing Crusade described it as being "as simple and natural as sitting in the sunshine". You do not have to make any effort; you are just there, in the sun, and you enjoy it. So it is with the Presence of God, and by making it complicated, you actually miss the joy of it.

From what I have written it will be clear that there are two approaches that may be called meditation. The first is a technique of some kind, where the meditator seeks to storm heaven's gate, and to achieve some part – or possibly the whole – of what is called in the religious languages of the world, enlightenment, realisation, satori, or the Kingdom of Heaven. However, even here, the enlightenment often occurs when the effort is given up. The other way is to be passive in our efforts, and to allow ourselves to be open to receive whatever wonders, illumination and joys that are the gift of the Higher Power, whatever we may call it. Both of these approaches are called 'meditation' by the religions of the world, and while the first – except in part – is not a part of the Quaker meeting for worship, the second definitely is.

Bradford Smith is quite clear that the Meeting for Worship is a significant part of the total picture of what meditation is. He makes the point more strongly than any other writer I have read by having two chapters in his book devoted to it. One is called 'Group Meditation' and the other, specifically, 'Quaker Meeting'. In fact, both chapters are about the

Quaker meeting for worship. In the first, he quotes the well-known and well-loved passage from Robert Barclay's *Apology* already given above. He goes on to quote Barclay again, in a passage less known and quoted, but which is extremely helpful in explaining the value of group meditation, and in particular the way in which a Quaker meeting can enhance the depth of the meditative experience.

> As iron sharpeneth iron, the seeing of the faces one of another, when both are inwardly gathered into the life, giveth occasion for the life secretly to rise, and pass from vessel to vessel. And as many candles lighted, and put in one place, do greatly augment the light, and make it more to shine forth, so when many are gathered together into the same life, there is more of the glory of God, and His power appears, to the refreshment of each individual; for that he partakes not only of the light and life raised in himself, but in all the rest.

Bradford Smith then goes on to talk about his experiences in the Quaker meeting in Delhi, where there were usually only a few Quakers present. The rest of the meeting was made up of Hindus, Sikhs and other Christians, and occasionally a Muslim or a Buddhist. Gandhi used to attend this meeting for a while during a difficult period of his life. One reason that this meeting succeeded so well is that silence is a universal language, and is in fact the greatest of symbols. The fact that a Quaker meeting is without visible symbols or techniques makes it a difficult experience for some. But for those who are prepared to let go of their preconceptions and allow the beauty and grace in the silence to speak to them, a Quaker meeting can be one of the most uplifting and enlightening forms of meditation.

Meeting for worship should be seen as a complement to individual practice. If Friends have found it difficult to talk about the meeting for worship, they have found it even more difficult to talk about their daily practice, or even to formulate it in a way that they can understand themselves. When I interviewed a number of Quakers for an oral history archive, this question of their spiritual practice outside the meeting was one of the most difficult, and some could not express it at all. Yet it was obvious from their lives and their presence that there was something that helped them through the rest of the week. The Friends who found it easiest to talk about their daily practice were those who had either borrowed something from another Christian tradition, or who practised some form of meditation, usually from Hindu, Buddhist or Sufi sources.

If these two – meeting for worship and individual meditation – are seen as complementary, and not set against each other, then it becomes easier to see their relationship. No longer is there any conflict, but each is seen as valid, practised in its rightful place. We can truthfully say, "Yes!

Meeting for Worship *is* a form of meditation, *and* it is a unique one, which has its own rules." Just as we would not want to mix, say, transcendental meditation with Buddhist insight practice, so at a Quaker meeting we should be firmly in the tradition of Friends, with surrender to the Divine as our only goal. If we hold the words of Robert Barclay in mind, as well as remembering the way in which silence can unite us beyond our words, then it should not matter if we practise any other form of meditation at other times; each will harmonise with the other.

However, even if we accept that Quaker Meeting is a form of meditation, and that techniques of meditation can have a place within it, we must remember that a Quaker Meeting is also *worship*, in the same way as a Christian *Eucharist* or a Hindu *Puja*. Worship is a celebration, which takes as its starting point the recognition of God as a power which is able to work in the world and in our lives. For Friends, this power is the power of Love, and in worship we recognise and surrender to this power so that it can become a living, guiding force in our lives. It is this combination of worship and meditation within a Quaker Meeting that is another aspect of its unique character.

CHAPTER 6

What of God?

The Language of God

ONE OF THE CHIEF characteristics of early Friends was their intimate and personal relationship with God. The religious thought of the day – as indeed with the majority of religious thoughts today – insisted that people could not know God directly, and that it needed the priest or the preacher to interpret God and His will for us. Quakers insisted – and still do – that each person can have their own direct relationship with God, and that it does not matter what race, sex or bodily shape a person has; there is still that of God within them, and God will speak to us if we take the time and trouble to listen. Our responsibility is to take that time, to be still and then to obey. In this attitude, Friends have found harmony with the mystics of all the great – and many of the lesser – world religions.

It would be tedious to give a long list of those writers who have pointed to a space within our being as the point where the Divine might be found. (some will be found in Appendix One at the end of the book) but it might be helpful to give one or two short examples from different sources.

The Kingdom of Heaven is within you. (Jesus)
God is nearer to you than your neck vein. (*The Qur'an*)
[God is] Closer than breathing, nearer than hands and feet.
    (Alfred, Lord Tennyson)
God is in thy heart. (*Guru Granth Sahib*)
The sage knows stillness in his heart, and all things happen,
    as if by themselves. (*Tao Teh Ching*)
Everyone has the Unborn Buddha Mind innately. (Bankei Zenji)
I, indeed, am the Self of all. (*Ribhu Gita*)

In the seventeenth century, the language that people could use to express their spiritual discoveries was very limited. It was basically the language of the Bible. There were probably a few people who knew the *Qur'an*, as there was a translation available, but they were very few. The rich language of, for example, the *Vedas*, the *Pali Canon*, the *Tao Teh Ching* and *Chuang Tzu* and all the other writings of the Eastern sages, were possibly less known to seventeenth century Christians than they were to those of the first and second centuries, when the trade routes between the Middle and Far East brought not only silks and spices, but spiritual teachings.

One of the great insights of Quakerism is that the life of the spirit requires two languages; the language of silence and the language of words. We have spoken about the language of silence in talking about meditation, though it is probably best to allow the Silence to speak for itself. Quakers have discovered that the best way for us is to gather as a group with the specific intention of worshipping God. However, this is by no means a unique discovery, as we saw in the first chapter.

Throughout their existence as a separate body, Quakers have evolved their own language of words to describe their spiritual findings. They stretched the boundaries of spiritual language, and I think it is fairly certain that if they had the riches of other spiritual seekers to draw upon, then we would have inherited a far richer tapestry of descriptive words. As it is, it is rich enough for most Friends. Today, the desire to describe spiritual experiences in a way that will be as truthful to our experience as possible, has led us to expand the language used. We use terms that are different from those used by early Friends, or we use familiar words in a different way. Phrases such as 'In the Life' , 'concern' and 'speaking to my condition', have been tested by time and are still in use. Because of this desire to express experience fully, and because Friends were generally not theologians, they tended to use ordinary terms in a special way to express clearly and simply what happens. However, traditional language does not always meet the needs of the latest discoveries of science, philosophy or even religion.

So the process continues today. For some Friends, the language of, say, the *Upanishads* or the *Tao Teh Ching*, expresses their feelings about God and their experiences in the Silence more clearly than is possible from just using the traditional words. For example:

It moves – yet it does not move,
It is far away – yet it is near at hand!
It is within this whole world – yet
It is also outside this whole world.

When a man sees all beings
Within his very self,
and his self within all beings,
It will not hide from him.[34]

Something there is without form and complete,
Born before heaven and earth,
Solitary and vast,
Standing without change,
Everywhere pervading all things,
Mothering all beneath heaven.
I don't know its name;
Not knowing its name
I style it Tao
And for want of a name call it great. [35]

Although the same is found in the Bible:

In the beginning was the Word, and the Word was with God, and the Word was God, the same was in the beginning with God. All things were made by him, and without him was not anything made that was made. [36]

Language changes, and many of the words used in the ordinary vocabulary would not be recognisable to seventeenth-century Friends, and vice-versa. Although today we keep some of our special terms – largely because of tradition and because they express much of what we wish to convey – the language of the spiritual life needs to be in tune with the times. Among other things we now strive to be non-sexist; not to imply prejudice in any way; and to be clearly understood by others who may not share our beliefs. Is it therefore not natural that we should wish to use the fullness of the spiritual vocabulary available to us provided it says what we want to say – even if it is associated with other faith traditions, and was unknown to early and even later Friends?

This is, I believe, an important aspect of the message that interfaith studies has to give to Friends today, and one which it appears that Friends are taking to heart. This does not mean, as some would suggest, that we have to leave behind the language that has been traditional to Quakers for nearly three hundred and fifty years. Far from it; we should be proud to use and share the terms that have expressed the essence of the Quaker Way over the years of our existence. But we can have both, and if one helps to explain the other to spiritual seekers, then this is surely good. If it helps us to meet with those who have found their Truth in other ways, that too can only be good for the world. After all, many wars have been fought over misunderstandings of religious belief. As Quakers we can surely realise that revelation comes first in silence, and then has to be put into words, and it is here that we need the combination of tradition with flexibility of language.

What kind of God?

Some years ago, at the Yearly Meeting held in Aberdeen, I gave a talk to the Friends Fellowship of Healing entitled, *What Kind of God, What*

Kind of Healing? which was later published by them as a pamphlet. It brought me lots of interesting correspondence from around the world. This title was inspired by a conversation which I had with a Friend, who was very puzzled about the question of God in contemporary Quaker thought. She had read many of the writings of early Friends, and felt at home with them. Among these Friends, God was a Living Reality, Presence and Power which could and did inspire, convince, heal and guide those who took the trouble to wait in the silence to find God's Presence. However, she discovered that, "Such language is all right and acceptable to Friends if it is within the pages of an old leather-bound book, but not if it is spoken at meeting". This has also been the experience of many other Friends.

She had been wondering if the language of other faiths had anything to say to Friends today, and found that when she quoted the *Upanishads* in meeting, even though the language was very similar to that of early Friends, it was readily accepted. She was also confused by the fact that it seemed to be acceptable among Friends to admit that they did not really know who or what they were worshipping. "What is happening?", she asked. I agreed that the wider reading of writings from other faiths might be of help, but suggested that an exploration of meditation and spiritual healing might offer her some answers. Then, in one of those apparent coincidences that have occurred many times in my life, I received the request to speak at the FFH gathering, and was asked for a title. "What kind of God?" was the first thought, and then, because of the nature of the meeting, I added the part about healing.

When I looked more closely at the problem of Friends who did not know who or what they were worshipping, I discovered something very interesting. It was true that many Friends admitted that they did not know anything about God, but they nearly always qualified it with saying, "But God is not this or that", or "Of course, we no longer believe that God is this or that". Although they admitted not knowing God, they thought they knew enough *about* God to know that He, She or It is not omnipotent, omnipresent, omniscient, all-loving or any of the other qualities that we have always associated with the Divine.

At this time, I had been reading the writings of a Korean Zen Master, Seung Sahn, who I had earlier heard give his first talk in England in Friends House. One of his sayings stuck in my mind. It was "Don't Know Mind is next to Enlightened Mind". I knew that in one way or another this was the message of many Zen masters. This "Don't Know Mind" is very different from the mind which seems to be afflicting the Religious Society of Friends today. It is not the mind which says, "I don't know ... but ...", admitting that we do not know about God, life or the world, but then adding that of course this or that must be true (or cannot be true). This is the "Don't Know Mind", which is prepared to let go of all the thoughts that we have ever had about God, both the positive and the negative ones. In my talk, I decided to explore whether God could be found in the 'Don't know!', and the result was that I found that many others were thinking along the same lines.

I wondered if this had any parallels in Christian or other writings. I discovered that it had. For example, I believe that this was the state of mind that George Fox was in when he heard the voice which told him that "There is One, even Christ Jesus, that can speak to thy condition". Many other spiritual teachers have come to accept that God cannot be described in any way, and that any description falls infinitely short of the Truth. When Jesus was asked by Pilate "What is Truth" he could only keep silent, as he knew that anything he said would be misinterpreted, even if it was believed. Apart from Buddhist writers, who mostly follow the Buddha in not even talking about God, there are many in other traditions who recommend the letting go of our concepts and ideas, so that we may truly listen to the still small voice which will tell us what we need. Christian classics such as *The Cloud of Unknowing* and the works of Meister Eckhart, Lao Tzu in the *Tao Teh Ching*, contemporary Hindu sages such as Ramana Maharshi and Nisargadatta Maharaj; and the great Sufi saint and poet Rumi, all tell us that we will only truly find God when we cease to create our own god in name and form.

The little modern Quaker classic *God is Silence* hints of this in the title. The author, Pierre Lacout, does not fall into the trap of saying that this is a definitive statement, but rather that he is trying to avoid adding new concepts to the old ones by giving "...the name 'Silence' to what others prefer to call 'The Word'". His reasoning is that:

> Speech tends to divide, people cling to words rather than to their meaning. Words give rise to religions, to churches which break up the family of simple souls, for whom loving worship should be enough, into rival sovereign fragments.
>
> Words split apart, Silence unites. Words scatter, Silence gathers together. Words stir up, silence brings peace. Words engender denial, Silence invites even the denier to find fresh hope in the confident expectation of a mystery which can be accomplished within.

However, we have also to find the words, for although there are a few people with whom we can really communicate in Silence, yet this is not possible for most of us. "Those who know do not speak, and those who speak do not know" said Lao Tzu. Yet many are grateful that he spoke in writing down the *Tao Teh Ching*, and that they have been enabled to find the True Silence of their being through his words. Pierre Lacout points to a possible reason, saying much the same thing even as he affirms that silence is to be greatly preferred to words.

If nevertheless I speak, it is to communicate with souls whose silence is in unison with mine and who hear the Silence of God in the words I use. If I speak again it is to awaken to this silence souls ready to receive it. But I am convinced that neither the written word nor the spoken word will ever be as precious as Silence. For in the soul dwelling in silence, God Himself is Silence.

Quaker Theology

The biggest problem for Quakers is to work out how theology relates to experience. When I was Manager of the Friends Book Centre (now the Quaker Bookshop) the Unitarians produced a study pack called *Building Your Own Theology*. I thought that this would be just what many Friends and meetings might be looking for, and I ordered a number of copies. I do not know how it sold to Unitarians, but Friends mostly ignored it, even when they were looking for study group material and it was pointed out to them.

This perhaps typifies the Quaker attitude to theology. It is not that they are indifferent to it, but for most Friends God is either a living Presence which they find difficult to talk about in words, (particularly since there are so many views of God in a typical meeting), or God is an unknown and unknowable force or energy which has a reality in their lives, but which they are equally unable or unwilling to articulate. One thing they are sure of is that the God expressed by most theologians is not the God that they know.

If you ask Quakers what they believe, it is almost certain that the answer will include the words "That of God in everyone". However, try to pin them down on exactly what is meant by this phrase, and you will find many different answers. Now maybe this is as it should be. It may be that the awareness of 'That of God' is a feeling, not capable of being pinned down to a physiological or psychological centre. It may be, and I believe it is, that the phrase is meant to carry overtones of almost every possible combination, so that it is more descriptive than saying, for example, that "God is found in each human heart". Perhaps we should leave aside such questions as "Where is 'That of God' to be found?", or "How much of God is to be found in 'That'?".

Here is an area where Quakers have a unique contribution to make, by recognising that our awareness of "That of God in everyone" is something that is at once an unknowable mystery, and at the same time a fact, the knowing of which has a practical application to our relationships with other people and the world in which we live. I would like to further suggest that we do not limit our realisation of this to people, but recognise that there is an aspect of the Divine in everything. This does not mean pantheism, in which God is in everything, but *panentheism*, in which the Divine can be found in everything, and also outside everything. In other words, not only is God found within us, but we are also found within God. Not only is God our very Life, but we are the very Life of God. Not only is God loving us at all times unconditionally, but God is the Love that we give to each other and to anything else that we love.

To help understand this mystery is where other faiths can help us, and have already helped many Friends. Within the Hindu tradition, it is common to speak of God as 'The Self'. They recognise the infinite unknowable Divine, and at the same time have a particular *form* of God that personifies the Divine and *is* the Supreme Form (with many hundreds, if not thousands, of possibilities, from human – male and female – to animal forms, and from mountains to abstract symbols). This form may be enshrined on an altar in your home or temple, and also seen as dwelling within your own heart, as being one with your True Self. It is worshipped with ritual and prayer, and is also sought in silent meditation within your own being. As well as your own particular object of worship, it is possible to recognise the forms of others as being equally valid for them, and to pay them due reverence. They are also accepted as forms of the One. This can also apply to the forms of God found in other religions.

In Islam and Judaism, the Oneness of God is emphasised, and the word of God as revealed in their holy writings is the guide for our daily lives. Both have their mystical aspects, and their sages have also taught that God is to be found within, as well as in and beyond the world. In their emphasis on the Oneness, they tend to exclude the various forms of God that are worshipped by other faiths. However, where the aspect of Oneness is put first it creates a meeting-point which can enable, for example, Hindus and Muslims to find common ground. Islam and Judaism also discourage the portraying of God with form, but are happy with the use of calligraphy as an artistic representation of that which they cannot portray. In this, they are like Quakers and Zen Buddhists.

Within Buddhism, there is little talk of God in any form. The Buddha refused to speculate about God, but instead pointed to the importance of the Way, that is, of practice and experience. Many Quakers feel at home with this, which is why Buddhist teaching and practice has had such an impact on contemporary liberal Friends. The Buddha outlined a pathway – the Noble Eightfold path – which laid down a way of life that was not bound by prohibitions, but rather emphasised a moral way of living that was to be undertaken for its own sake; because it was the wise and skilful thing to do in order to harmonise relationships with the world and those living in it.

It would be easy enough to find many quotations to emphasise all this, but I feel that the following from Harvey Gillman's semi-autobiographical Swarthmore Lecture, *A Minority of One*, exemplifies what many Quakers feel about God.

> I do believe that there is a power which is divine, creative and loving, though we can often only describe it with the images and symbols that rise from our particular experiences and those of our communities. This power is part and parcel of all things, human, animal, indeed all that lives. Its story is greater than any one cultural version of it and yet it is embodied in all stories, in all traditions. It is a power that paradoxically needs the human response. Like us it is energised by the reciprocity of love.

A suggestion

In former times in Japan it was the custom for disciples to challenge their teacher to write in a few words, often in a poem, or, at the most, on a single page, the essence of his teaching. Some of the most wonderful poetry and clear teaching has come out of this practice, and I have found it a good one.

Look for a moment at the language that you use to express your spiritual life. Is it the same language that you use everyday, or do you have a special 'sacred language' for describing your relationship with God? It is not wrong to have such a special way of talking about our inner life, but it is also good to try to express it in everyday language, even if we only do it for ourselves. Take a page, and, slowly, in longhand (no word processors, please) write down what you have actually come to *know* regarding your spiritual life. You do not have to show it to anyone, but it is good to keep it and meditate on it from time to time. Keep it for a year, and then do the same thing again before comparing the two. Even if you find it difficult to keep a journal, comparing what you have written will help you to observe the pattern of your spiritual life.

Note that I said "life" and not "progress". This exercise is not meant to encourage comparison. Rather, it helps to close the gap which can arise between the spiritual and the everyday, and it also helps us to articulate the essence of our spiritual lives. The ideal that the everyday is spiritual is an integral part of Quakerism, and our language has an important part to play in that. As we notice the changes in our spiritual language, we will be more easily able to accept the influence that the writings of other traditions and practices may have on us.

CHAPTER 7

Coming Together

IT IS HARD TO KNOW what percentage of members of Britain Yearly Meeting have been influenced by, or practise some kind of meditation taken from a tradition other than the Christian, but indications are that it is fairly high, particularly among convinced Friends. If you then add those members who are – officially or otherwise – in dual membership with some other Christian body, the number may be as high as half, with the number of attenders in similar positions higher still. From my experience in talking to Friends, I would say that the reason is not because of any inadequacy in Quakerism, but is due to the growing acceptance among seekers today that no one religion or tradition can provide all the answers that we require throughout our changing and increasingly complex lives.

India: More from Ramakrishna

There is a story of Sri Ramakrishna, the great Indian saint of interfaith practice, who, when asked why he practised a number of traditions in order to find God, replied that he didn't want to eat his fish curried every day. Sri Ramakrishna, who had a profound influence on many Friends, explored a number of different methods to realise God, embarking on each with an open mind and an acceptance of the Truth as found within that tradition. Though he accepted this Truth, he wished, after the manner of a spiritual scientist, to prove each one for himself.

Within his own Hindu tradition he first developed an intense devotion for the form of God as the Divine Mother, and he affirmed that the Mother appeared to him and taught him many things. Under Her guidance he practised meditation, and came to realise Her as One with the whole of creation. This led him to periods of ecstatic samadhi in which his consciousness was lifted out of the world. But he also desired to see for himself if other forms of God were as real, and whether other methods of practice would lead to the same goal. Still within Hinduism, he practised what is called *Dasya Bhava*, the surrender of a perfect servant towards his master. Then, under the guidance of a teacher who was led to him, he practised tantric disciplines in which God is experienced and worshipped as Power (*Shakti*). One result of this is the development of extraordinary psychic powers which can enslave many and lead them away from the goal. Though he developed these powers, Ramakrishna was not deceived, and knew that his achievement of the goal was only due to the grace of the Divine Mother. He came to see the female form as God, without thoughts of sex or physical attraction.

Ramakrishna practised all the other possible relationships of the devotee with God, and also the formless practice of Vedanta, from which he went on to experience the Nirvana of the Buddha, and affirmed the Truth of the Buddha's noble path. Next he took up the practice of Islamic mysticism in which he worshipped God as Allah, the Compassionate Ruler of the universe. In this he was helped by a Sufi mystic who was also guided to him. In this practice he completely abandoned his Hindu prayers and meditations, and ceased to attend the temple. Instead, he went to the nearby mosque, and said prayers in the Muslim fashion five times a day. He spent a final three days in intense prayer, and was able to confirm that the Path of Islam is a valid path to God.

Ramakrishna also worshipped Christ as an incarnation of the Divine. Again, he forsook the Hindu temple and his usual practices. He read the Gospels, and the personality of Jesus came to be a reality for him in this way, not through the mediation of the church. We could almost imagine him hearing the voice that spoke to George Fox. He developed a strong desire to learn for himself the truth about Jesus and his mission. One day, he was gazing at a picture of the Madonna with the child Jesus, when he felt rays of light coming from the picture and enveloping him. For the next three days he lived in the presence of Christ, convinced of His Reality and Divine state. At the end of this time he saw the figure of Jesus approach, embrace and merge with him. He lost ordinary consciousness, and entered into a state of spiritual trance. At the end of it he was convinced that Jesus was a Divine Incarnation, and he maintained a deep devotion to him for the rest of his life. Even today, the centres of the Ramakrishna Order celebrate Christmas and Easter with services and meditation. As we have seen in a previous chapter, there were other links between Ramakrishna and Quakers, and certainly many Hindus who have supported Quakers in their work were influenced by him.

Ramakrishna's influence has also come to Friends in another way. As with Misra, quoted earlier, there have been others who have become deeply involved with his teachings, and yet have remained in membership of the Society of Friends. Margot Tennyson was a member of the Vedanta Centre, and frequently went there to meditate and gain spiritual counsel from Swami Bhavyananda, the head of the Centre, whom she acknowledged as her teacher. I also attended the Centre when it was in London, and it was there that I first met Swami Tripurananda, who, as a *sannyasin* of the Ramakrishna Order and a member of the Society of Friends, has had a great influence on the interfaith work of Friends, and in particular the activities of the Friends Interfaith Group.

Swami Tripurananda was literally born into Friends, as his parents were wardens of Bedford Meeting House at the time of his birth. He grew up within the meeting, and has acknowledged many times the deep influence that the elders of that meeting had on his early spiritual development. He was involved with Young Friends, and with the marches and non-violent demonstrations against nuclear weapons. Though he believed passionately in the cause, he could not shake the feeling that, for him, political activity – however well-meaning – was not the answer. He also felt doubts as to some of the orthodox Christian teachings.

When he came to London as a student, he visited various groups to see what they had to offer, and among them was the Ramakrishna Vedanta Centre, which then had premises in Muswell Hill. There he met the man who was to become his teacher, Swami Ghanananda, at that time the head of the Centre. While he could understand little of this first lecture, he knew that here was someone who had something that he wanted to share. Eventually he moved into the Centre, though with no thought of eventually becoming a monk. He developed his meditation and his learning under the guidance of the Swami, and eventually went to India.

In a talk given at the FIFG gathering at a Yearly Meeting, he called the next years "the eastern side of my spiritual quest". Friends encouraged him rather than the reverse, and he freely acknowledged their help and blessings. After some years as a novice, he again went to India and became a fully ordained member of the Order. But he always retained his membership of Friends, and still feels himself a member of his meeting, even though he is mostly unable to attend. In this, he was encouraged by his superiors in the Order. In his talk he emphasised this.

> Many people say to me, "Why did you become converted to a Hindu?" "I haven't", I reply. "Actually I'm a Vedantist and a Quaker". My Indian friends find no contradiction in a *Swami* [an Indian monk] being a Quaker. But the invariable response of Westerners I happen to meet who pose the same question is one of considerable surprise, if not disbelief. In the fifteen years that I have been a member of the Ramakrishna Order I have not heard one word from my Superiors, read one *sloka* in the *Upanishads* or *Bhagavad Gita*, which runs counter to my pre-monastic days spent in the company of Friends, attending Meeting for Worship and playing my role as any other young Friend.[37]

It is fascinating to speculate on the possible karmic links between Quakerism and the Ramakrishna movement. It might seem that when Ramakrishna welcomed and blessed Misra, and when Misra openly acknowledged Ramakrishna's status as a great soul, something was set in motion which has continued through the ages. Certainly, Quakers have cause to be grateful to the Centre, which has always been a place where Friends could go and feel at home (though some found difficulty in the shrine-room, with its picture of Sri Ramakrishna as the external object of worship). The Friends Interfaith Group held several meeting there, and both Swami Tripurananda and Swami Bhavyananda were always willing to lead groups for meditation and discussion. There were also some other Swamis in the USA and India who had close links with Friends.

India: Gandhi, Tagore, Marjorie Sykes and Quakers in India

The second major source of inspiration for Quakers from the Hindu tradition came from the life, work and teachings of Mahatma Gandhi. Gandhi's emphasis on *ahimsa* (non-violence), on simplicity in living, and on the experience of the Divine within all living beings has been an inspiration to Friends. This is still the case today. Quaker insistence on the same things must have also inspired Gandhi when he first met them and came to know of their beliefs.

Marjorie Sykes was known as a 'Quaker Gandhian'. Indeed, her biography written by her friend Martha Dart is called just that. She was born in 1905, and went to India in 1928 to teach at a school for girls in Madras. She soon became influenced by Gandhi, particularly by his ideas on education. She had introduced some similar ideas in her school, and later added some of the others. There was a small Quaker group already meeting in Madras, in the homes of some of the members, and Marjorie began to attend. There she began to feel the depth of the Spirit in the silence, and later spoke about it.

> As we sat together the outward silence deepened into inward stillness and a loving unity which might or might not find expression in simple spontaneous words. This was a different spiritual discipline from individual morning meditation but the practice of each kind of stillness helped the other immensely.[38]

Later, on her first visit back to England, Marjorie became a member of the Society of Friends, but the essence of her Quaker understanding and work was always within an Indian context, where she was always ready to relate to those of other faiths who were prepared to meet with her in silence. Her biographer puts it this way:

> She responded to the Quaker belief that in all human beings of whatever race or creed, there is something that enables them to recognise and respond to 'Truth', 'a Light Within', 'an inward teacher'.[39]

65

Marjorie was to become identified in some way or another with most if not all the Quaker work in India. She was invited to join the staff of Santiniketan, Tagore's school in Bengal. The vision that Tagore had was typified in his poetry. In one verse, which had inspired Marjorie, he says:

Day and night, Thy voice goes out from land to land
Calling Hindus, Buddhists, Sikhs and Jains around Thy throne
And Parsis, Muslims and Christians.
Offerings are brought to Thy shrine by the East and the West
To be woven into a garland of Love.[40]

Later, Marjorie became more involved with Gandhi, and with the whole work of Friends in India. She always saw this as a two-way process. When writing her first book, *Quakers in India*, she summed up this ideal in a letter to Friends.

I want to emphasise that I am just as interested in the impact of India upon Quakers, as of Quakers upon India. Because of this, I express my hopes to myself in thinking of this study as one of Quaker 'encounters' with India, one of a two-way traffic of ideas and influences.

Her life was a testimony to this attitude right up until her death in 1995. She lived a life of true Quaker simplicity, which she did not see as a negation, nor as a withdrawal from the world, but as a "...full and clear-sighted involvement...", which led her to become fully involved with the needs of the ordinary people of India. She was always dedicated to education, but this was not just book-learning. For her, education included awareness of the spiritual dimension of life, of non-violence, and of the high purpose of manual labour which should not be denigrated or thought inferior to learning.

In a stunning article in *Friends Quarterly* in 1956, Marjorie expressed what she saw as the fundamental business of religion and for me summed up the whole basis of Quaker inter-faith work. This purpose she sees as helping us to "...*grow into saints*". This sainthood is not a negative condition, nor is it an excess of piety. It is to dwell "...in the life and power of God". She goes on to say:

The Saints belong to the world, they are the exclusive possession of no tradition. "The saint", says the Christian scholar C C Martindale, in a striking phrase, "*has been* a Christian". One could say equally truly, "The saint *has been* a Muslim, *has been* a Hindu, *has been* a Buddhist". He has reached, by one of these pathways, the goal of life. The path is not the goal.

Those of us who are still on the journey need the paths. The Society of Friends is one path, for some of us it is our path. But the goal is the life of the saints in God, a life not of passive "sinlessness", but of overflowing compassion, of humble service, of inward power and peace....

Is not the secret of fellowship between adherents of many faiths that each should be able to see the others as fellow-travellers, by varying paths, to that same goal? What other permanent basis of inter-religious fellowship can there be?[41]

Quakers and Sufism

Although many Quakers are 'unitarian' rather than 'trinitarian', it is only recently that I have become aware of Friends who are influenced by the mystical teachings of Islam as found in the Sufi traditions. This does not mean that there have not always been those who have discovered these teachings, particularly as found in the mystical poetry of Jalaluddin Rumi and other Sufi poets. The essence of their teachings is found in this idea of the Oneness of God, and His mercy and compassion in giving to us the possibility to know him more deeply and eventually to lose ourselves in Him.

This is well illustrated in the following poem by the great Sufi poet Shah Abdul Latif, who, like Rumi, had disciples of several different religions.

Say God is One; learn not another word.
Write that True Word in the tablet of your heart.
Call Him not a Lover nor a Beloved either;
Call Him not Creator nor the created either;[42]

Early Friends also had links with Sufism in the form of the story of *Hayy Ibn Yaqzan*, originally composed by Avicenna, first translated into English by a Quaker, George Keith, and included in early editions of *Barclay's Apology*. This story is of the mystical journey of Hayy Ibn Yaqxan, who:

...without converse of man, and living on an island alone, attained to such profound knowledge of God, as to have immediate converse with Him, and to affirm that the best and most certain knowledge of God, is not that which is obtained by premises promised, and conclusions deduced; but that which is enjoyed by conjunction of the mind of man, with the Supreme Intellect, after the mind is purified of its corruptions, and is separated from bodily images, and is gathered into a profound stillness.[43]

This simple truth, which most contemporary Quakers take for granted, deeply alarmed some people at the time. Simon Ockley, the Vicar of Swavesey, who also later published a translation of the story, added a thirty-six page appendix to refute the idea that anyone could arrive at ultimate truth through the action of their own inner light. In it, he attacks what he calls,

...this fundamental error of the author "that God has given such a power or faculty to man, whereby he may, without any external means attain the knowledge of all things necessary to salvation, and even the Beatifick Vission (sic) itself. ...[44]

It might be thought that Quakers would be perfectly happy with such an 'error', but it was London Yearly Meeting of 1846 that had the passage about Hayy Ibn Yaqzan deleted from later editions of *The Apology*. Their minute said in part:

... We think it is probable that the scholastic form of the work [*Barclay's Apology*] may have been one means of leading the author to pursue some doctrines too far, and to exceed the safe limits of spiritual forms of expression.[45]

Quakers and Sufis both seek to find God in the stillness within, but it is not only in the mystical contemplation of the Divine that there is an affinity between Sufism and Quakerism. Both seek to include the physical and mundane world with the spiritual, and not to find a separation between them. Neither of them have priests, nor are their teachers set apart. Sufi teachers do not normally earn their living from their spiritual teaching, and they are expected to have a trade or profession to cater for their everyday needs. While they have meeting areas where they gather, these are not usually kept solely for that purpose. For example, I know of one Sufi group which meets in a school in the evenings after the pupils have gone home.

On the surface then, it would seem that the Sufi path is one which might appeal to Friends. That it has only done so in a small way is, I think, due to lack of knowledge, and to the fact that many Sufi groups are not open to non-Muslims. Even those that are do not, by and large, have open public meetings or centres where anyone can go to learn meditation or other spiritual practices. Sufis have been among the Muslims who have attended Quaker meetings in India and even in the UK, but I think I would be fair in saying that there has not been the same degree of involvement by Quakers in this tradition as with Buddhism and Vedanta.

Judaism

From the very beginnings, Quakers have had definite links with Judaism. Both Margaret Fell and George Fox wrote books especially addressed to the Jews, although the main aim of the latter was to seek conversions to Quakerism. Margaret Fell used language that her readers could understand, quoting from the Old Testament, avoiding mention of Christ, and encouraging them to turn away from outward religion to the Light of God in their hearts and the Inner Spirit. Some of these were translated into Hebrew.

In more modern times, Friends have been members of such groups as the Council of Christians and Jews, both nationally and locally. These groups discuss very deep theological issues, not shirking the differences, but working together in a spirit of Love and understanding. Their meetings, which have included prayer and worship, have often been held in Quaker meeting houses.

My own experiences have been almost exclusively with the Reform or Progressive aspects of Judaism. Jews from these traditions have been happy to share in Quaker worship, and we have found much common ground in dialogue. I remember attending Quaker Meeting in Richmond, Indiana, which was held in the local synagogue, as the meeting house was being re-built, and hearing of the deep friendships that resulted from this generosity of the local Jewish community. A delightful story was told to me by a member of my own meeting, who often visits and eats with Jewish friends. At meals, they are happy to share a Quaker silent grace, and on one such occasion their little girl asked what she should be thinking of in the silence. "Think of those people who do not have enough to eat" was the reply; one which I am sure Friends would be perfectly happy with.

In 1981, the Friends Interfaith Group invited Rabbi Jeffrey Newman of the Reform Synagogue in Finchley, London, to be the speaker at our Yearly Meeting Gathering. His talk, entitled *In the Light of Experience*, was one of the three that we chose to publish in our pamphlet *Three Spiritual Journeys*. He had said from the beginning that he did not wish to give a formal talk, but to have a sharing experience with Friends, and this is what happened. He allowed spaces where he listened to comments from the group, and he was disarmingly frank about his own upbringing and his early attitudes to Judaism and Jewish people. Even after all this time, reading his talk brings back the memory of a very real and human interfaith dialogue which, without pretensions, managed also to leave a deep feeling of shared spirituality.

Before the talk, he had attended a session of Yearly Meeting, and was very impressed with the Quaker business method. He confessed to having learned something about silence from Quakers. In the comments from the audience, it was clear that this sharing was indeed a two-way effort as several speakers acknowledged the influence of Jewish spirituality on their lives. Remembering all this, I suppose it should not have been a great surprise to learn that Rabbi Newman's synagogue has a group which regularly meets, partly in silence, to explore many aspects of spirituality.

Early in 1999, Harvey Gillman led a weekend at Woodbrooke on the relationship between Quakerism and Judaism. The weekend turned out to be extremely helpful for many of those attending, who had become Quakers and rejected their Jewish background. While they are happy with much that Quakerism offers, with the rejection of creedal statements and theological formulae, some had found difficulty when they had come across a strong Christological emphasis. Out of this weekend came a publication, *The Journal for Jewish Quakers*, which at the time of writing is in its third issue. (There is also a similar American publication, *The Old Foundations*.) It is obvious that the relationship between Quakers and Jews is something that is going to see many further developments, and it is hoped that will prove to be a fruitful and healing experience for all concerned.

Sikhs, Jains, Zoroastrians and Baha'is

There are a number of other faiths which Friends have had contact with over the years, particularly here in the UK. The Sikhs are not a small group, and the British Sikh community is the largest outside India. Jains and Zoroastrians are relatively small groups, although there is a wonderful Jain temple in Leicester.

I have not personally come across Friends whose spiritual practices have been influenced by teachings from these groups, but a number of their ideas have had an impact on the beliefs of individual Friends. For example, the Jain attitude to non-violence, not only towards people, but to the whole of the world and all who live in and on it, is very profound. Jain monks and nuns give an example in their everyday lives by such actions as wearing masks, sweeping the ground as they walk and filtering drinking water. It goes without saying that they are vegetarians, and many are also vegans.

Zoroastrians and Sikhs share with Quakers an attitude of not separating the material from the spiritual life. Although their ways of worship are vastly different, they also have an attitude of treating work as worship, and doing all things for the glory of God. Zoroastrian teaching is primarily dualistic, but definitely had an influence on early Christianity, and thus on some Quaker thinking. They would certainly have understood George Fox's 'Ocean of light and ocean of darkness'.

Sikhs do have a reputation for being warlike, but this is not all that it seems. Certainly in its early days, Sikhism was non-violent, and there are some Sikh traditions which maintain this attitude even today. It is probably significant that one of these, the Namdharis, are a group that has worked closely with Friends in interfaith activities over the years.

The Baha'is also share many beliefs with Quakers. The newest of the "world religions", they accept the Unity of God, and the truth of all God's prophets, that is, the founders of the great religions. They believe in progressive revelation, and the value of science. This means that they have much in common with Quaker Universalists. Baha'is do not have a

70

separate priesthood, and give equal rights to men and women. They advocate universal education, and are opposed to all forms of prejudice. They are tireless workers for peace, though they are not pacifists, believing in the value of a world peacekeeping force as part of world government. They have co-operated with Friends in many interfaith activities, and it is true to say that their ideals have made a deep impression on many of the Quakers who have worked with them.

Taoism

When we come to Taoism, we have a different picture. It is probably not Taoism as such which has influenced Quakers, but rather one book, the *Tao Teh Ching* (pronounced, and, today, sometimes written, *Dao Duh Jing*). I have been amazed over the years by the number of Friends who have a copy of this book on their shelves, and by those who have read it and even know it well.

As mentioned in the Introduction, the *Tao Teh Ching* is probably – after the Bible – the most translated scripture in the world. There have been well over a hundred editions in English alone, to say nothing of those in French, German, Dutch and other European languages. When I was Manager of the Friends Book Centre in London (now called the Quaker Book Shop) I must have sold more than ten different translations. There are translations direct from ancient and modern Chinese, versions from people who have compared a number of different editions – what Arthur Waley calls "scriptural translations" – and books that are related to the original in tenuous ways such as *The Tao of Pooh, The Teh of Piglet, The Tao of Healing* and even *The Tao of Management*.

For Quakers, I suppose that one of the most significant events in our relation to this book was the publication of the translation of Herrymon Maurer, who is a American Friend, and who had previously written a fictional account of the life of Lao Tzu, original author of the *Tao Teh Ching*. His version was entitled *The Way of the Ways; Tao*, and was published in the USA by an interfaith group called Fellowship in Prayer and later, by Wildwood House in the UK.

Herrymon Maurer says of his translation that it is the result of living with the *Tao Teh Ching* for over forty years, and that, in the words of the King James Bible, it is "translated out of the original tongues, and with the former translation diligently compared and revised". In his notes, he often compares the *Tao Teh Ching's* words and sentiments with those of the Gospels, and with Quaker writers such as John Woolman, George Fox, and Isaac Penington, and with a number of Jewish Hassidic writers such as Martin Buber.

Among the reasons that the *Tao Teh Ching* has had such a profound influence on Quakers is its attitude to violence, its emphasis on seeking that of the Divine within ourselves, and its appreciation of the feminine in the spiritual life. Lao Tzu tends to prefer feminine qualities to masculine ones, and when he personifies the Tao, he calls It 'Mother' rather than 'Father'. Lao Tzu also teaches the value of silence and stillness in our lives. He also emphasises the value of occasionally 'doing nothing', which, he tells us, does not mean that nothing gets done. "The Sage knows stillness in his heart, and all things happen as if by themselves". Quakers, with their busy lives, need to be reminded that sometimes waiting in the Divine Stillness is better than leaping into immediate reaction.

I have lived with the *Tao Teh Ching* for over thirty years. I am fairly sure that I got my first copy – probably Arthur Waley's translation – before I joined Friends. I suspect that it was just after I had discovered Buddhism, when there was an enthusiastic appreciation of all things oriental. I now have more than fifty editions on my shelves, still use it as a source of meditational material, and try to be guided by its wisdom. I know of many Friends, and of many mystically inclined members of other faiths, who find an equal inspiration in its pages. Perhaps because of its brevity, or because it does not appear to be advocating any other specific faith tradition, or maybe since it has a special atmosphere all of its own, the *Tao Teh Ching* seems to have a special place in the mystical literature of the world.

Another source of the appeal of the *Tao Teh Ching* is the way in which it both explains some of the mysteries of creation, and yet emphasises the great paradox by saying clearly that such things cannot be explained. It provides answers which seem to be more than speculation, yet the chief answer is to point us to the stillness within, where all things are eventually resolved. It possesses an inner stillness, which appeals to the busyness of the Western Quaker mind, which knows intuitively that, however much we may try to change the world, there are some things that can only be changed by leaving them. Such sayings as "The only way to clear muddy water is to leave it alone", convey their essential truth, which many Friends find, is an antidote to their fundamental busy-ness.

The *Tao Teh Ching* also expresses non-violence, but in a way that is different from Friends' usual approach. It was written at a time of warring states in China, and part of its purpose was to help rulers to come into harmony with what we might call "The Will of God". In addition to the development of inner stillness referred to above, the idea of "naturalness" in thought and action is encouraged, which will allow rulers to be generous of spirit with those they might otherwise have crushed. The best rulers are those who are invisible, and who allow the people to get on with life in a simple and natural way. It is inevitable that comparisons are drawn with the Sermon on the Mount, and it is often said that the *Tao Teh Ching* helps us to understand practical ways in which the principles of this essential teaching of Jesus may be lived.

Quakers and other Christian Traditions

One of the interesting things about interfaith work with Quakers, is that our personal relationships with other Christian bodies tend to be treated in much the same way as our relationships with other faiths. There are many members and attenders in Britain Yearly Meeting today who are regular attenders at another place of worship, and are even in dual membership. Reasons for this may vary between a feeling of loss occasioned by the lack of music or ceremony in Quaker worship, a need for spoken prayer, or for a clearer Christian theology than is found in most meetings. Other people have come to Friends because of the need for silence, or because of our Peace Witness, but do not feel that they wish to completely desert a religious community where they were happy, even if it did not provide for all their needs. In fact, we even have one or two full members of the Society who are still in holy orders.

There are Friends who are completely unable to understand these attitudes. Such Friends have been known to object to an applicant for membership because they have not completely left their previous church. They may even find it easier to understand a Friend who attends, for example, Buddhist meditation, than one who is still involved in another branch of the Christian Church, particularly one where sacramental worship is the norm. Some American meetings will not tolerate any suggestion of dual membership, and will not allow a person to join if they have not completely left their previous church.

This, of course, comes out of the traditional Quaker attitude to the other Christian Churches, and to priests and all forms of sacramental worship. However, things are changing. In spite of some opposition, Quakers are now full members of the 'Churches Together' movements, having been let in by a special clause which does not demand a creedal statement, but only that we adhere to the spirit of that statement. Some Friends have not been happy with this, but in general Quakers today are ecumenically minded. For some this has meant becoming active in their local church councils, and even serving as officers. This in turn has led to objections from a few fundamentalist Christians – some even referring to Quakers as "a cult". I feel that all this ecumenical activity is good for interfaith work. Where Quakers can be open to traditional Christian language it helps us to remember our roots, while Quaker openness to other languages will help Christians in general to become more accepting of other faiths.

Quakers and the New Religious Movements

Writing about those who think of Quakers as a 'cult' reminds me of an incident in which I was personally involved. In the September 1993 edition of the *European Christian Bookseller's Journal* there was an article on "Cults" written by Doug Harris of the Reachout Trust, which is an evangelical Christian organisation devoted to combating new religious movements. The article was reasonably fair – though inaccurate in parts – but what was of particular concern to Friends was that we were included in a list of cults given in the second part of the article.

I responded to the article with a letter which was printed, and I was interested to see that others wrote in similar vein. I said that I did not think that Quakers should be listed as a cult, and explained that we do not fit with any of the points which the writer had outlined as typifying a cult. Among these were authoritarianism, belief that a particular group taught the only true way, and emphasis on appealing to the weak-minded. I said that Quakers certainly were not authoritarian, definitely did not believe that there was only one spiritual pathway, and that we encouraged freedom of thought.

We are now living in a time which some call 'The New Age'. One of its main characteristics is a great increase in the number of people who express a belief in the Inner Light or the Christ Within. Some of these follow 'channelled' teachings, which are said to be brought through from a higher spiritual source, and many of these teachings emphasise what we would call 'That of God Within'. Some of these teachings demand slavish obedience to the person at the head of the group, but there are others which emphasise that each person must follow their own Light. We can only know them by their fruits. Most of these groups teach some form of meditation, and with the coming of the millennium, these teachings are becoming more public.

Many of the groups that are arising at this time share with Friends a respect for creation, a commitment to non-violence, encouragement of simplicity of lifestyles and recognition of the equality of men and women. Some are also opposed to the idea of a priestly caste, and share decision-making and the work of the group equally among the members. On the reverse side, there are groups which have little or nothing in common with Friends. Even so, all need to be acknowledged and considered fairly and openly.

What should be the Quaker attitude towards such groups? Where we find among the New Religious Movements those that equally reject the cult criteria, and where they seek to live up to similar ideals to our own – recognising, as we do, that they do not always succeed – then I feel it is important for us to do three things. Firstly, we need to encourage honest verbal communication, so that we understand each other clearly and know what are our similarities and our differences. Secondly, we should be willing to work with them to achieve common aims. Finally, we should seek to encourage deeper understanding through the practices of mutual irradiation or something similar, so that we share in silence with those for whom it is similarly important.

Regarding groups with whom we have little or nothing in common, we still need to be open to dialogue in the same way that we might with political groups which do not share our views. Here again, honest verbal communication is important, and we must be clear what the distinctive witness of Quakerism actually is. Not only meditation, but mediation also has its place in interfaith work. We may find that, although we take opposite views on most things, there are matters about which we agree. If we are asked to co-operate with them in areas of work, we need a great deal of clarity and discernment before agreeing, so that it does not look as though we are advocating something that is against Quaker principles.

We can have problems where there are Friends who are emphatically opposed to a particular point of view, but also where there are Friends who have a common interest, but lack those with whom they can discuss it. A good example was a recent weekend on *Quakerism and the Pagan Traditions* which was held at Charney Manor. This arose out of a genuine concern to approach these traditions in the same way as we do Hinduism or Buddhism. Because of the pressures from the larger churches, Pagans have for the most part been excluded from mainstream interfaith work. We hoped that the mutual irradiation approach might be helpful. Unfortunately, we had considerable opposition from some Christian Friends, but in the event it was not they who caused problems with the weekend itself. What happened was that the weekend was more or less taken over by some Quakers who also followed Pagan teaching and practices, and who wanted an opportunity to celebrate together. While this was not necessarily a bad thing, it did mean that the purpose for which the weekend was conceived – which was the result of a genuine concern – was not fulfilled. This does illustrate a problem. Anyone who undertakes interfaith dialogue in this way needs to be very sure of the people who are taking part.

Many spiritual seekers from the 'New Age' already dialogue with Friends, and some of them use our meeting houses when they do not have premises of their own. Some individual Friends also draw spiritual sustenance from such groups. I feel that we need to be more aware of them, as some may be new movements of the Spirit, just as Quakers were in the seventeenth century. We need to avoid pejorative statements, such as the negative use of the term "Pagan" , and not be put off by the views of other Christians. We must apply the Quaker principle of finding out such things for ourselves, and not judge just because of a label or reputation. This may become more necessary as some of these groups become our partners in opposing the rise of fundamentalist thinking, which seems to be growing as people more and more demand certainty in matters of belief.

Conclusion

It is not always easy for those Friends who have chosen to add to their Quakerism the beliefs, language or practices from another faith tradition. On occasion I have been told by such Friends that they feel isolated at their meetings, and that they have nobody with whom they can talk or share. In short, they feel that nobody will listen or try to understand why a particular teaching or practice has come to be an essential part of their spiritual lives. They had expected that Friends, so open in many things, would express sympathetic joy on hearing of their discoveries. Instead they are either told that such things are not Quakerly, or they are ignored.

Informal Quaker groups such as the Friends Interfaith Group, The Seekers and the Quaker Universalists have fulfilled a very real need in providing a time and place where such Friends feel they can communicate with others who will understand. It is to be hoped that their work does not appear to other Friends to be breeding division. I know that this is not the case. It is just that Friends who find it easy to relate to others in this broad spirituality will naturally come together. Others are not excluded, but if they do not speak or understand the language used, then they will not feel at home.

We all have the potential to "... hear where words come from", and it is in the Quaker tradition to do so. It is vital that we learn to practise this tradition, if the increasing influence of other faiths on the spiritual lives of Friends is to be a harmonising rather than a disrupting factor of contemporary Quakerism. We have plenty of examples. I pray that we may learn to follow them, *and at the same time* be equally open and tolerant towards those Friends who find their spirituality naturally expressed in orthodox Christian terms.

CHAPTER 8

Quakers and Buddhism

IF VEDANTA AND India provided one of the great sources of influence from other faiths on Quakerism in the early part of the twentieth century, possibly the major one for the new millennium is Buddhism. Looked at from one perspective, it is difficult to know why this should be so, as there are many basic differences, and, from the viewpoint of Christianity, Buddhism might be said to be the most 'alien' of all the world's faiths. However, many philosophers and religious people have endorsed the statement by Arnold Toynbee that the most significant influence on the twentieth century is going to be the way in which Christianity and Buddhism have related to each other. Readers will have gathered that I have a particular personal relationship with Buddhism, having been a Buddhist when I was accepted into membership of the Society of Friends. I still see myself as a Buddhist, though not in opposition to the Christian roots of Quakerism. For these reasons, when it seemed right for this book to have a chapter looking in depth at the relationship of Quakerism with one other world faith – other than Christianity, which has been done many times – Buddhism was the obvious choice.

Over the years, many Friends, learning of my deep interest in Buddhism, have confided to me that they too have been influenced by it to a greater or lesser extent. This applies not only to Quakers, but to many other Christians as well. I will list some of the beliefs and practices which Friends have told me have appealed to them. (Comments in square brackets are additions which have come from Friends, while the words in italics are my own comments.)

- Buddhism is essentially experiential [and so is Quakerism].
- It does not ask us to believe those things which we find impossible to believe [and neither does Quakerism].
- It does not talk about God [and I find talk of God difficult]
- It does not talk about the Soul [another subject that I find difficult] (*this from people who see "That of God" as different from the classic conception of the Soul*)

- It has practical techniques of meditation (*probably the most popular reason*)
- It does not matter that I continue to be a Quaker (*this would not be true of all Buddhist groups*)
- It is non-violent like Quakerism (*mostly true, but not in all cases*)
- It is closer to science
- It has a different view of 'sin' from the classic Christian one
- It is more tolerant in matters of sexuality and sexual orientation
- It does not have 'eternal hell' (*Buddhism does have hells which are every bit as horrible as the Christian ones, but they are not eternal*)

This is a fairly comprehensive list, though not an exhaustive one. Friends who are attracted to Buddhism usually have a combination of reasons.

Facing differences

In relating to any other faith – and possibly to Buddhism more than others – it is important to face up to the differences as well as to accept the similarities. Everything may seem harmonious on the surface, but when we go deeply into another faith with a view to adopting it in tandem with our existing one, there will always be problems. In looking at the ways in which Buddhism and Quakerism can co-exist in the spiritual life, there is a need to acknowledge those aspects of Buddhist thought which are not harmonious, and which will have to be faced. I will try to do this in a positive way, taking account of the various comments, questions and criticisms which have been made to me by Friends over the years, particularly at courses, conferences and retreats with the theme of Quakerism and Buddhism in which I have been involved.

There are three aspects to this consideration. Firstly, we have the Friend (or attender or enquirer – the same points are true for them as well) who feels attracted to Buddhism, but who knows little about it. For these people, learning about Buddhism is a part of their spiritual journey. They may take some of the meditation techniques and acknowledge the ethical basis of Buddhist thought. However, their need is for a learning process, and they have not arrived at any firm position with regard to their interest in Buddhism.

Then there are the regular attenders at Quaker Meeting who also practice Buddhist meditation, or who may even regularly visit a Buddhist centre. In spite of freely acknowledging the help that they have found from Buddhist sources, they primarily think of themselves as Quakers. One of their principle needs is to come to terms with the fact of having to go outside of Quakerism to find something to fill the gaps in their spiritual lives. They need to reconcile the various teachings in order to satisfy their intellectual questioning, and to respond to comments from Quakers and others who do not understand why this should be necessary.

Finally, there is the serious student of Buddhism, who is quite happy to be considered both a Buddhist and a Quaker, though probably *not* a Buddhist-Quaker or a Quaker-Buddhist (most of us think there are no such animals). Such Friends have wrestled with the problems, and are perfectly happy in blending the two together within their own journeys. However, when faced with intense questioning from those who cannot understand how this is possible, they may find difficulty in explaining their position.

An experiential religion

One of the principle reasons that Quakers are attracted to Buddhism is the shared view of Buddhism and Quakerism as both being experiential. By this I mean that both religions are perceived as giving proven value to the experience of the individual. This was the reason which first attracted me. In the *Kalama Sutta* the Buddha is quite specific in urging his listeners to value their own experience.

Do not accept anything simply because it has been said by
    your teacher;
Or because it has been written in your sacred book;
Or because it has been believed by many;
Or because it has been handed down by your ancestors;
Accept and live only according to what will enable you to see
    truth face to face.[46]

This is one good basis for beginning the study of Buddhism. In order to follow this teaching, we need to look carefully at what we do believe, to see whether it is real for us, and whether we have *experienced* it as true, helpful and likely to lead to harmony, or whether it is just based on creeds that we still recite – even if not literally – through habit. (This is not to say that creeds cannot be true for us; the test is whether we can honestly say that we have experienced their truth for ourselves.)

We also need to bear in mind that there are many varieties of Buddhism, with differences every bit as great as those found in Christianity. These range from the apparent simplicity of the Theravada (Teaching of the Elders – mostly coming from Thailand, Burma or Sri Lanka) to the complex symbolism of the Mahayana (Greater Vehicle – found in China, Tibet and Japan). Within this latter tradition there are many sub-divisions, ranging from the ritual and visualisation of the Vajrayana (The Diamond Path of Tibetan practice), to the iconoclasm of Zen. There are also problems when only a part of the teaching reaches the west. For example, within Zen, many of the early writers present it as being a path that is austere in the extreme, so that Westerners going to Japan were amazed – and often shocked – to find that Zen practice has its fair share of chanting, bowing and other ritual.

In my life I can honestly say that I have experienced the truth in the teachings of both the Buddha and Jesus. Basically, we have in the words of either teacher the essence of what the Buddha called "the Holy Life". However, many schools of Buddhism have grown out of later teachings and commentaries on the basic texts, and what is considered basic in one is not necessarily true or relevant in others. We have also to remember that the combined scriptures of the two main schools of Buddhism, the Theravada (the Pali Canon) and the Mahayana (Sanskrit and Chinese scriptures) are many times the size of the complete Bible. Also, they are often written in oriental poetic styles which means there is constant repetition. Buddhists, particularly of the Mahayana traditions, may be asked to believe or accept things that are much more difficult than the Virgin Birth, the miracles, the Atonement, or the Resurrection. Certainly, if we take the Mahayana scriptures literally, we find many far more amazing events described. But such things are not always what they seem.

A good example of a teaching which is not immediately obvious or logical, occurs in the three scriptures of the Pure Land schools of the Mahayana. In these scriptures, claimed as revealed in a mystical manner by Shakyamuni, the historical Buddha, but in fact found to have been written many years after his death, we are told about another Buddha who lived millions of years ago. This Buddha is called *Amitabha* (Infinite Light) or *Amitayus* (Infinite Life). Before he achieved enlightenment under another even older Buddha, he vowed to create by the power of his enlightenment a special land, where those who recited his name could be born, and where there were no barriers to enlightenment. There, "Even the birds sing the Dharma (teaching)", we are told.

Taken literally, this is a charming myth, which the more logical mind at first finds it difficult to believe. Indeed, one Western scholar has said that "If Amitabha Buddha lived when the scriptures say he did, then he must have been a dinosaur". However, if we look deeper, we find that the guidelines of the *Kalama Sutta* are applicable even here. For one thing, according to the scriptures, this Buddha *is* Infinite Light, which shines unhindered throughout the universe. The beginning of *The Gospel of St John* in the Christian *Bible* tells us that the Light shines in the darkness, and that the darkness cannot grasp it. Quaker tradition tells us that George Fox saw an ocean of Light, which swallowed up an ocean of darkness, while many other mystics in the world's traditions also tell of this Light that is everywhere, even within us. Thus, the truth of this experience is expressed in story form, which could be given to people who could not read or write, but who could easily learn to memorise and recite the poetic form in which this scripture is presented.

The concept of Infinity is not an easy one to grasp, even in this present scientific age. To have it spoken of clearly some two thousand years ago is staggering, and many of today's scientists are just beginning to appreciate the reality of the experiences outlined symbolically in the scriptures of the East in terms of worlds within worlds, and of the existence of the vastness of the universe. More than that, these scriptures point us to something that is beyond even the stretched imaginings of scientific speculation. This is why scientists like David Bohm and Fritjof Capra have been able to engage in fruitful dialogue with mystics and spiritual leaders such as the Dalai Lama and J Krishnamurti.

This and many other examples show that Buddhist scriptures – just as with the Christian variety – should not always be taken literally. Some of the Buddha's teachings, such as the *Kalama Sutta* mentioned above, his teaching on mindfulness and the Noble Eightfold Path, are expressed in clear unambiguous terms, even in English translation. However, particularly in the Mahayana, there are scriptures (and commentaries on scriptures) which are tortuous in the extreme nature of their symbolism, and were never meant to be taken literally. Such scriptures are only helpful if (a) the symbolism speaks to us, and/or (b) if we have a teacher who has penetrated to their heart, and can not only explain them, but be seen to live their truth.

Spiritual teachers

When we come to consider spiritual teachers there is an additional and potentially more serious problem. In Buddhism, the teacher is often seen as requiring a degree of respect and obedience which involves the suspension of the disciple's reason and even conscience. The student must accept unquestioningly almost anything that the teacher does or says, if they tell us that it is for our spiritual welfare. Some Buddhists even go so far as to say that their living teachers should be viewed literally as the Buddha himself, and the teachings reinforce this view.

This is not something that Quakers can easily accept, and, to be fair, neither can all Buddhists. My former Zen teacher told us quite firmly not to accept anything that we could not believe, and used to play occasional jokes on us by making statements that were just too much for us to accept. (The question about believing in "The horns of a hare" is one of the classic *koans* – nonsense riddles which lead beyond the mind – of Zen Buddhism). He would, however, always own up, and then invite us to make up our own minds using both reason and intuition. He pointed out that the Buddha encouraged the use of reason up to the point where it was no longer helpful. The Dalai Lama has recently said that Westerners are much too naive towards teachers, and that they have not only a right, but a duty, to test teachers before accepting them. He was also very firm in saying that they should not do anything that conflicted with the demands of conscience.

This concept of exaggerated respect paid to teachers may manifest in various forms. A basic one, which many Quakers have problems with, is in the area of bowing. Bowing is a traditional form of respect in the East, and in many traditions it is considered quite normal for a student to perform a full prostration towards a teacher, or even towards a picture of the teacher. This bowing has a ritualistic aspect, and is described by some teachers as being a spiritual exercise for the uprooting of pride. It is expected even from newcomers. Other teachers have a more open attitude, and only demand it from committed disciples, while still others will allow it from anyone. I remember taking a friend to consult a very learned and revered Tibetan lama. When we arrived, he was sitting surrounded by several dogs. While we were trying to find a space in which to bow, he sprang to his feet, shook our hands, and then placed cushions against a wall. Not until he had ensured our comfort did he sit down and ask why we had come. I later learned that he would never allow ritual respect such as bowing, except when he was in full robes at a formal ceremony.

There is a story of a Westerner who visited a Buddhist temple, and watched with disdain while the monks bowed to the Buddha image. "What's all this bowing" he said, "I thought Zen had nothing to do with it. I spit on Buddha images". The old abbot could scarcely conceal his mirth, but, putting on his most serious face, looked the visitor straight in the eyes and said in his most sonorous voice, "You spits, I bows". The teacher who first told me this story went on to say that he still thought bowing was a good spiritual exercise to assist with the removal of the sense of ego. However, as with any spiritual exercise, it needs serious co-operation and awareness if it is to be helpful.

The whole question of the power and authority of Buddhist teachers has caused a number of severe problems, with teachers accused of the abuse of students. Where the press has got hold of such stories, this has not been good for Buddhism. Several years ago there was a conference held on this subject, and I was asked to be present to bring the perspective of Quaker experience to the discussion. In the discussion, it was pointed out that not all schools of Buddhism give this sort of exaggerated respect to teachers, many of whom are happy to be likened to "fingers pointing to the moon". In another context, someone expressed the thought that the ideal teacher was "someone who wanted nothing from you". I think Quakers would be happy with that.

Techniques of meditation

The other principle reason why Quakers are attracted to Buddhism is because of the practical methods of meditation that are taught. Many Buddhist centres have open classes teaching meditation, and there are many books available detailing the various practices. These usually start with a basic awareness of the breath, which has the function of allowing the mind to become quiet, while not trying to force it – which is almost impossible – to do so. Because the breath is so fundamental to our existence as human beings, it is a perfect way to begin meditation, being free from most of the concepts which accompany other ways.

In Buddhism, watching the breath, which is based on specific teaching of the Buddha as found in the Pali scriptures, is accepted as a valid form of meditation in its own right. It is also used a first step for other more detailed and complex forms of meditation. Similarly, many Friends have found it a perfect way to help still the mind at the beginning of Meeting for Worship, while recognising that it is not worship itself and, like the raft used for crossing the river, can be left on one side as the gathering of the meeting deepens.

Other forms of Buddhist meditation are *vipassana*, where the meditator watches the action of thoughts and feelings as they move across the screen of consciousness. This kind of awareness also has a place within Friends' worship, though again not as an end in itself. We need to be aware of the thoughts and feelings that come to us in worship, and seeing them clearly, enables us to discriminate between our own desires and a genuine impulse to minister.

There are also many forms of visualisation, mostly from within the Tibetan traditions. These are not recommended for general practice, and normally require some kind of initiation or empowerment. They should only be practised under the guidance of a teacher who has used them successfully for many years, and who has been authorised to teach them as a part of a recognised lineage. This also applies to some extent to formal Zen meditation, although it seems on the surface to be the extreme opposite of the Tibetan forms. None-the-less, it is interesting to note that both these traditions are considered "short" or "direct" forms, which, properly practised under an enlightened teacher, can lead to enlightenment in this very life.

One other type of Buddhist meditation, which involves some visualisation, as well as the peaceful mind developed through awareness of the breath, is *metta* (loving kindness) meditation. Some people feel that this is the basic and deepest practice in Buddhism, and one derived directly from the teachings of Shakyamuni Buddha. In this, we consciously project loving kindness to all, to ourselves, to those we love, to others we know, and particularly to those we hate or resent. We wish them well, often using the traditional phrase, "May they be well and happy". Finally, we extend these thoughts to all beings, and even to the earth itself. This has similarities to the Quaker practice of prayer by holding people in the Light.

Buddhism also teaches us new ways of looking at the nature of the self, with its constant change, and encourages us to enquire whether it is a reality at all. The Buddha taught that one of the three signs of being was "*anatta*". This literally means "not self" but is often taken to mean "no self", with the interpretation that the Buddha said that there was no such thing as a "self". In fact, the meaning is that the self is not any of those things that we mistakenly think that it is. If we can define it, then it means that we have not grasped it, and indeed, the truth is that the self cannot be grasped or defined. In this is it like the Tao as referred to in the *Tao Teh Ching*.

All these techniques of meditation offer new ways to still the restless "monkey mind", and are often very attractive to Friends. They find that they offer something that is complementary to meeting for worship, and which helps them to practise ways of stilling the mind in their daily lives. This daily practice blends well with the process of centring down in meeting for worship. As has been pointed out earlier, this is good, so long as it does not take over the whole of the time of worship. I know Friends who are so entranced by meditation practice that they forget or ignore the wonder of Quaker worship. This is sad. I have seen such Friends sit in meeting in meditation posture on the floor, obviously giving their whole attention to their breathing or whatever practice of meditation they are involved in. I have even occasionally seen the use of a Buddhist rosary. It becomes obvious that they are not surrendering to the grace of the shared Inward Light which is God's gift in Meeting, and are trying to achieve everything by their own efforts. Quaker worship and Buddhist meditation *do* complement each other, but in worship it is our relationship with God and with the other Friends present that is of prime importance. Friends who feel drawn to use Buddhist or other forms of meditation in meeting for worship need to remember this.

Buddha and God

Many Friends find it difficult to understand how a religion that does not speak of God can be allied to a tradition in which the Living Presence of God is one of its foundations. Here I can only speak for myself. Other Friends may have different ways of reconciling these two apparent opposites, and for them it may be that Buddhism's reluctance to speak about God parallels their own. For me it was – and is – the other way round. In my early days of Buddhist practice, I became convinced that God was a reality for the Buddha, but that his realisation was so deep and profound that he would only speak about those things that God is not. I was fortunate in my teachers. My first Zen teacher (he would not allow us to call him 'Roshi' or 'master', though he was) had much the same attitude, not speaking about God except to say that whatever we thought God to be was probably true, but definitely not the whole story. Other teachers that I have had were all happy with Buddhism and Christianity, with the Buddha and with Jesus and God. I have also been fortunate to come across the writings of R H Blyth, Frederick Franck and the wonderful book by Jamshed Fozdar, *The God of Buddha*, all of whom have helped me to become happy with the idea of God and Buddha living side by side in silent harmony.

As I have said earlier, if Jesus Christ and Gotama Buddha were to meet, there is no doubt in my mind that it would be in the deep silence, and that they would not waste words on idle discussion. They might laugh together, particularly at the ways in which learned commentators and committees have misunderstood their words. They might even weep together for the same reason. I am as certain as I can be, both from studying the teachings of both masters, and from what I have intuitively felt about them, that there would be a deep harmony between them. The scriptures of both Christianity and Buddhism are based on their dialogues with those they met, and I feel sure that both were able to discern the spiritual state of the questioners before they even opened their mouths, and that their teachings were given accordingly. Although we now have only the four short books of the life and teaching of Jesus, at one time there were many more, and the range of the teaching recorded extends from the deeply symbolic and esoteric – almost tantric – writings of a text such as *Pistis Sophia*, to the short pithy Zen-like sayings of the *Gospel of Thomas*. The full range of the gospels and other writings termed "apocryphal" or "Gnostic" compares very favourably with those of the Buddhist Scriptures, and many Friends are now investigating such of these writings as have survived.

Early Quakers were also given to mystical visions, and they often expressed them in deeply symbolic language which was ground-breaking at the time, but which was richer and more scriptural than Friends would use today. Quakers have also had their quietist times, where they have looked towards an inner glory that they were unwilling to put into words. They have also had their evangelical phases, where they have wanted to shout the gospel message from the rooftops. With modern Friends open to whole ranges of new language, it is not surprising that the language of Buddhism should provide a fertile medium to express spiritual truths which some feel are outside the experience of mainstream Christianity.

When the Buddha refused to talk about God, it was only because the depth of his experience was such that there were no words that were suitable. The Buddha found that to use any terms for God meant that his message would be misunderstood. Jesus' silent response to Pilate was for the same reason. The Christian writer J B Phillips summed it up in the title of his well-known book, *Your God is Too Small*. The Buddha had a vision of the Divine that was greater than the known universe, and contained more possibilities than the mind could envisage. Quakers too have had this experience, and while some have been content to use the existing Western language of religion, others recognise that it is too limiting.

Buddhist/Christian Dialogues

For the past ten years I have been a member of a Buddhist/Christian Dialogue Group, which has met twice a year. The group consists of about twenty each of Christians and Buddhists, from a variety of traditions. It is the direct result of a concern felt by Tom Gulliver, a Quaker who was a member of the Friends Interfaith Group, and for some years the Honorary General Secretary of the World Congress of Faiths. The Group is very much a 'heart' group, and we always begin with one member – either Christian or Buddhist – leading a meditation.

Each meeting has a theme, and this is usually introduced with short talks by two speakers, one Buddhist and the other Christian. Topics have ranged from 'Spiritual practice' to 'God and Emptiness'; from 'Service in the world' to 'The importance of Church or Sangha'. The introductions are given from the personal experience of the introducers, as they are there for themselves, and not as official representatives of any particular group. Following the introductions, there is usually a "bring and share" vegetarian lunch, followed by open discussion. The group closes with a time of silence, following which it decides the theme for the next meeting.

As with many such groups, the most important aspect is probably the shared lunch and the opportunity for deep friendships that it creates. However, in the group meeting, the fact that we open with meditation means that there is a deep sense of sharing, which allows for honesty and openness in the discussions. Differences are not shirked, and there is no attempt made to avoid discussion of issues that might be controversial.

This group is very precious to those who have been privileged to be members for some time. In it, through stillness, honesty and deep friendship, difficulties are resolved, and each participant finds spiritual strength for their life's journey. The coming together of what fundamentalists might think of as irreconcilable differences is a living illustration of the Love of God – or Infinite Compassion – and it is That which expands our own faith in ways that might not otherwise be possible.

For me personally, it has been a tremendous source of spiritual strength and clarity. It helped me to reconcile the two aspects of my spiritual life, and to see clearly that they are not opposites. Some of the participants are Roman Catholic priests, and I feel that, had I been able to meet some of them when I had my difficulties with that Church, I might never have left it. Although the group members are invited because they are clearly from one faith or another, most have considerable experience with the other tradition. There are priests who practise Buddhist meditation, while Buddhists work closely with Christians in various forms of service to those who are disadvantaged. I remember one Roman Catholic priest saying something that has stayed with me, and which was in itself a healing experience. He said; "It is wonderful to be either a Christian or a Buddhist, but there is one thing better than either. It is to be both".

This was wonderful to hear, for, in spite of difficulties and misunderstandings, I am happy to be both a Quaker and a Buddhist, but not a Quaker Buddhist or a Buddhist Quaker. To be both a Quaker and a Buddhist means for me that I acknowledge the Christian roots of the Society of Friends, without which it would not be the body that it is. I also respect and share the Quaker insights regarding the nature of God, and the practise of Worship. At the same time, the Buddha's teaching of the Infinite Light of Buddha Nature amplifies that of the Quaker doctrine of the Inward Light, while the words of the *Kalama Sutta* which meant so much to me at the beginning of my spiritual search are still vitally important to me. The teaching of Jesus is something that "...helps me to experience Truth face to face", and thus I respect and try to live by it, not finding anything that conflicts with the Buddha-Dharma. Remember that Jesus told us that he was not interested in those who called him "Lord, Lord", but rather in those who do the will of his Father, God.

"Don't know!"

The final area where Buddhism is helpful to Friends is that it allows us to say "I don't know" with full honesty and openness when we are faced with the mysteries of life. In the chapter about God I spoke about the influence of the Korean Zen master, Seung Sahn, and how one of his sayings: "Don't Know Mind is next to Enlightened Mind" impressed me deeply. I first heard this at a meeting that he addressed in Friends House, London. For him, as indeed for many Friends, it is not just something negative to say "I don't know" when faced with ultimate questions regarding God, the problem of evil, and the nature of humankind. I have already referred to the publication of *What Kind of God, What Kind of Healing?* As a result of this, I received many letters thanking me "... for giving permission to say 'I don't know'". I had not thought at the time that this was what I was doing, and indeed I still wonder, but it is interesting that so many Friends saw it this way.

A typical letter said:

For many years I have sat in my Meeting, feeling that I was the only one who didn't have any real knowledge of what is meant by "That of God within us", or of the real Presence of God in my life and worship. I felt that all the other Friends had deep and real spiritual experiences, particularly in meeting, and I have felt unable to share my doubts, even with my closest Friends. Elders suggested that we use your pamphlet as the theme for our annual discussion group, and, lo and behold, I find that there are many others who feel the same as I do. Thank you for providing a way in which we can share our doubts.

Grateful as I was to receive this letter, I was also shocked. I had not intended that this should be a way in which such negative feelings could be voiced, but rather to indicate that being able to honestly say, "I don't know" is a very positive opening of ourselves to true prayer. And, for me, this came out of my knowledge and practice of Buddhism. It was only later that I was to realise that such a way of positive denial is also part of the Christian, and even the Quaker tradition. Christian mystics such as Meister Eckhart and the writer of the *Cloud of Unknowing* (the title should have given it away) were quite clear that this is a valid Way to God.

This was known to the Zen Buddhist tradition for hundreds of years. Great revelation, *satori*, enlightenment, is preceded by great doubt. The acceptance of this doubt opens the way for Divine Grace (though Zen Buddhists would not express it that way). Hakuin Zenji, the great reformer of Japanese Zen once said; "Small Doubt, small enlightenment. Great doubt, great enlightenment". Some Zen masters deliberately fostered what they termed "The great ball of doubt", but it is not necessary to do this in an artificial way. Indeed, it may be dangerous to do so if the student is not living in close contact with a master who has had deep personal experience of this Way.

Life itself brings the doubts, the problems, the koans, and all that is necessary is to learn to say "Yes" to Life and to God, and to accept that there are things that are beyond the human mind to grasp. In his wonderful book on living Zen Buddhism, *The Goose is Out*, W. J. Gabb tells us:

I move and have my being in a Zen monastery which I call the world. Around me are all the other monks, the human inhabitants of this planet, many of whom are still ignorant but some of whom I recognise as enlightened in their degree.

In this monastery, I am subject to privations, austerities and hard work, with little leisure and long vigils. I move amid beauty and horror....

Daily I meet the Master who presides over this community of mankind, and hourly I ponder the problems he has set me to solve. Some of them are koans which are not capable of logical solution, but all admit of an answer. Sometimes, all too frequently, the Master slaps my face. Occasionally I return the blow. And sometimes, when I least expect it, he brings me tea and cake.

Who is this Master? When I was in the womb he overshadowed me, and ever since I left it I have turned to him instinctively as a babe turns to the mother, not knowing the nature of the relationship but clinging to the breast.... I know him simply as my life.

I know that many Friends can identify with this. In the Meeting for Worship we often experience a similar relationship with life. In Christian terms it is surrender to the Will of God, which is often beyond us, for God's Ways are not our ways.

It is in the Silence that Quakerism and Buddhism can meet in Oneness. Both teach us in different ways to go beyond language, and once we have learned to do this, then there is a deep stillness in which the Divine Presence, the Unborn Buddha Mind, is experienced. Out of that stillness, which takes us beyond our personal concepts and ideas, there is a coming together which is paradoxically experienced as more real because of the differences between the approaches of the two faiths. There may not be many Quakers who would want to call themselves Buddhists, yet the influences of Buddhism on the faith and practice of Quakers will continue to grow, quietly and subtly. However, what is not usually appreciated is that Quakerism is also having an effect on Buddhists, and I know of a small but increasing number of Buddhists who regularly attend Quaker meeting, who are inspired by the Quaker attitude towards helping to bring peace and harmony to a suffering world, and who find their '*Sangha*' (community) among Friends.

In an earlier chapter I mentioned Professor Yukio Irie who came to speak to Friends at Yearly Meeting gathering. He had come from a Zen Buddhist background, but in spite of becoming a Quaker he had retained a great deal of respect for Zen. While here, he gave us a copy of his translation of Hakuin Zenji's well-known *Song of Meditation*. (Hakuin was one of the most famous of Zen masters). It is too long to quote in full, but after many verses in praise of Zen meditation, the final verse says:

What could you desire then?
Since Absolute Rest is in you,
Wherever you are, you are in the Kingdom of Heaven,
And you are Buddha just as you are.

And, in a deeply gathered Meeting for Worship, Quakers also find that we are 'That of God', 'The Living Christ' and the 'Pure Inward Light'. This is why I feel that there are close links at the deepest level between Buddhism and Quakerism, and that the exploration of these will eventually enrich both.

CHAPTER 9

What of the Future?

Here and Now

AT THE TIME THIS book is being written, Friends are engaged in a number of new initiatives in the Interfaith field. *The Celebration of Universal Love*, Margot Tennyson's last great concern, has just been celebrated, and a full account can be found in Appendix 2. Such celebrations are by no means the whole story, but they are a very important part of coming together for greater understanding and co-operation. If people can celebrate together, they can worship together, and if they can worship together, they can also meditate together. Celebration, worship and meditation together comprise three of the five major aspects of interfaith understanding. The other two are studying together and working together.

As I said earlier in this book, it is often difficult to know the precise degree of involvement of Friends in interfaith work, because so much of it goes on quietly in local meetings. This is particularly true in the areas of study and work. For example, many Friends are involved in committees and groups of various kinds to do with education. Most Quakers, even those who are not otherwise involved with interfaith matters, will be clear that in matters of education it is important to know as much as possible about those who are our neighbours. And if our neighbours have a different faith from ours, with different festivals, practices and ways of worship, then our children need to be aware that these are not something alien to react against, but an opportunity for shared celebration. This can only happen if we know something about the reasons and beliefs underlying the differences.

Quakers are also involved locally in many aspects of community relations, and here, too, there is often an interfaith dimension. Quaker meeting houses are used by a variety of groups for religious and cultural gatherings. This often brings Friends into contact with members of other faith communities, and may in turn lead to invitations for Friends to attend religious gatherings. Quakers are known for the lack of symbols in their meeting houses, which are therefore seen as neutral territory. To my certain knowledge Quaker Meeting Houses have provided homes – temporary or permanent – for groups of Buddhists, Hindus, Sikhs, other Christian groups, Jews, Moslems, Baha'is, Spiritualists, and groups who practise meditation, yoga, T'ai Chi Chuan. There may be many more. Friends are also known for their willingness to listen to both sides of a problem, and so they may be called in to mediate in disputes. All this will continue, and indeed may be one of the most useful contributions that Quakers make to the multi-faith world in which we all live, a view which to my certain knowledge, is shared by many people of other faiths.

The Quaker Committee on Christian and Interfaith Relationships (CIR)

This Committee and its work have been mentioned earlier. It was asked by Meeting for Sufferings to co-ordinate all aspects of official Quaker work in the Interfaith field. It meets twice a year, usually for a whole weekend. The main thrust of their work is ecumenical, dealing with such difficult areas as the Quaker membership of the Council of Churches in Britain and Ireland (CCBI), Quaker relationships with the other Christian Churches (national and local), and with the World Council of Churches. The Committee's huge workload includes not only discussion on a large number of reports, meetings, and theological issues, but also practical work that is clearly within Friends' testimonies, such as the abolition of torture and work with refugees. All this generates a great amount of paperwork, and takes a lot of time. The Committee also offers guidance to the Society of Friends on such issues as Quaker attitudes to the sacraments in ecumenical worship, and produces supporting literature.

It will be clear from even this brief summary of the Committee's work that the time it has available for interfaith work is severely limited. Most of the bodies that it works with have their own committees or groups dealing with the relationships with other faiths. The Committee regularly receives reports from them, and is concerned not to duplicate work that is already being done by these other groups. Work such as that with refugees obviously carries more weight with government if all the religions can speak with a united voice, and here the interfaith dimension is most helpful. Although Quaker insights are often helpful in shaping attitudes, a separate Quaker response – with extra costs and wasting of our limited resources – is not needed, and may, in fact, prove counter-productive.

Another area in which Quakers are working with the other churches is in the field of opposition to racism. There is considerable agreement that education is necessary to aid this process, which means that an understanding of other faiths is an essential part of the educational system.

Quakers have consistently voiced their support of this, and have had some influence on it, both nationally and locally. The Quaker testimony against all forms of racism clearly includes religious intolerance, and although I have no real knowledge of the number, I suspect that there are many Friends working locally and quietly in furthering this concern.

CIR are trying to work out an interfaith theology, and one of the results of this is that three papers on the subject were printed in *The Friend* of 30th May 1997.[47] It is important for Friends to be clear on their attitude to the theology of interfaith. Quaker presence in groups of Christians looking at such questions as interfaith worship and religious pluralism can and does help to balance the influence of the more fundamentalist members, and it is good that Quakers have a voice in such discussions. However, if Quakers are seen to be too open to ideas of spirituality other than the traditional Christian ones, this can have a reverse impact, marginalising Quakers in relation to churches which have a more evangelical component. I am not sure if this was anticipated when CIR took over interfaith matters.

Theological speculation will meet the needs of only a few. Those of us who have been involved in this work for many years know that the real need is in the daily lives of Friends who have incorporated some inspiration from other faith traditions in their spiritual practices. A number of questions need to be asked. Why do Friends feel that they need spiritual practices or views from other traditions? Is it because Quakerism, for all the beauty of its meeting for worship, does not provide the means to fully satisfy the spiritual hunger felt by many who come to it? What does Quakerism provide in terms of *daily* sustenance? What is the deepest meaning of 'the spiritual life' for Friends today? Can – as Gandhi suggested – a Hindu, Buddhist or Muslim become a Friend just as easily as a Christian? What implications does this have for Meetings?

I hope that the committee will not want to re-invent the wheel, and will consider carefully what role mutual irradiation and similar approaches might find in answering these and other important questions. There need to be times when these questions can be faced, with all their difficulties, in a spirit of reconciling worship. Most of the interfaith concerns of Quakers today are to do with themselves as individuals, their practices and beliefs, problems of their relationship to other Friends in their meetings, and their need to get together with others who will at least understand the spiritual language that they wish to use. In whatever way the Committee is guided, I hope they will bear this in mind in their future deliberations.

Let us take as an example the question of reincarnation. Some years ago, a conference on this subject was suggested. It was not found possible to incorporate it into the mainstream activities of London Yearly

Meeting (as it was then), or at Woodbrooke, but a space was found for a conference at Charney Manor. It was thought that probably only a few Friends would register, but, as far as I remember, the Manor was almost full. It was a lively, searching and supportive conference, and the one thing that came out above all was that Friends who believed in reincarnation – as possibly the only thing that for them would explain the inequalities of life in terms of a God of Love and justice – were mostly afraid to talk about it at their meetings for fear of the reaction of other Friends. I wonder how many meetings have ever had – or would dare organise – a discussion group on reincarnation?

Looking at the work that CIR has done over the last few years, I am sorry to say that it seems to me that they have lost an opportunity. Instead of building on the work of the Friends Interfaith Group, and the unique contribution that Friends such as Douglas Steere and Margot Tennyson have made to the process of interfaith understanding, they appear to have approached the subject from the academic, theological and bureaucratic considerations which govern the attitudes of other churches. They also seem to have – perhaps inevitably – allowed themselves to be influenced by the demands of ecumenism, giving weight to what other Christians will think if Quakers are too open to ideas and practices from other faiths.

However, as I have demonstrated in earlier chapters, such ideas and practices are already here, leavening the spiritual lives of many Friends. These Friends are looking for support and dialogue within the Society and are not finding it. They need CIR to be able to give them help and advice in their personal and corporate spiritual journeys, and it is to be hoped that the Committee will be sensitive to the needs of such Friends. This will be very difficult if the membership of the Committee is not drawn from Friends who have experience in the deep sharing which comes out of practices such as mutual irradiation.

What can we learn?

It is important in a survey such as this to consider what Quakers might learn from other faith traditions. Individual Friends have already taken aspects of belief and practice from other faiths, and have benefited greatly, even if there have been some difficulties on the way. In addition, Friends have gained much from the expansion of their spiritual language in being able to use terms that reflect twentieth century life and scientific discoveries. It might be useful to look at those aspects of world faiths which can expand Quaker life and thought even further.

We have seen how Buddhism takes the relevance of experience one step further, even encouraging its followers not to believe or accept things that cannot be said to make their lives more peaceful and harmonious. Meditation is one of the chief vehicles through which this can be achieved, and through which aspects of life that have hitherto only been beliefs, become for us living facts. Other world religions similarly have key factors which might help us to expand our spiritual lives.

Islam makes much of the unity of God, and shares with Quakerism an awareness of God as compassionate and merciful, in other words, a God of Love. In order to extend this awareness, there are certain practices enjoined on pious Muslims. One of the chief ones, as far as Quakers are concerned, is that of regular prayer throughout each day. I am sure that Quakers could learn much about the spiritual life if they too decided to have five (or more) short times of prayer or worship throughout the day. In those times, we could become aware of the Divine presence within ourselves and others, and ask for nothing more than a deeper awareness of that presence and the ability to listen to and obey God's voice.

Hinduism – insofar as it can be viewed as a single religion – also teaches us of the basic unity of God, but does so in a way that seems diametrically opposed to that of Islam. While Islam refuses to allow God to be pictured with form, Hinduism not only allows it, but encourages us to find God in a multitude of forms, including human and animal. In this way, we learn that God is present *within* all aspects of creation, as well as being *above* and *beyond* them all. Hinduism also recognises a huge variety of worship, including the silent way which Quakers have made their own, and recognises that each is valid. Along with Buddhism, it teaches the recognition of karma and rebirth, and enables us to view the actions of others within a cosmic rather than a local perspective.

In becoming involved with all this study of other faiths, Quakers should not forget their own Christian roots. It is often easier for some Friends to find good things within, for example, Zen or Vedanta, than to gain inspiration from Anglicans or Roman Catholics. Yet we must remember that we come from the same roots, namely, the life and teachings of Jesus. If it seems to us that these have become lost in the welter of theological mis-interpretation or church politics, we still have the Gospels in common. Other churches have perhaps been quicker to recognise this than we have, hence the invitation to join the Churches Together organisations. However, if we need reminding, then we should look towards the Christian mystics, and the practical work in the world of such bodies as Christian Aid.

We should also remember that these days other Christians are often more at home with silence than we are. It is true that their worship is not silent, but Friends who have shared retreats with other Christians will know that many of them have more experience with meditation and individual silence than Friends. At such gatherings, I have often noticed that Quakers are the ones who find the most difficulty when they are deprived, not only of conversation, but also of reading matter, and particularly during such activities as silent meals.

Other religions can teach us the value of community, of mutual support in times of trouble. This is something that Friends used to be very good at, but which seems to have become lost from some of our meetings. It is true that other traditions often have the advantage of paid clergy, around whom such work can be organised. But Quakers can still learn from the way in which shared ideals can inspire a caring attitude, particularly towards those members of a meeting who may not have the advantages of being part of a larger family unit. In earlier times, even when there were large extended Quaker families, a meeting became an additional network through which the various sufferings of Friends could be addressed. Some of the other faiths – and other churches – have maintained this, and there is much that we can learn from them.

We also have to learn that we cannot always have a specific Quaker response to everything that goes on in the world. Some of the smaller faiths have realised this, and have concentrated their resources on those areas where they can make a unique contribution which is unlikely to be matched elsewhere. They encourage their followers to support existing organisations in areas where they have an interest but lack the resources to make a difference. Such 'wise stewardship' used to be a feature of Friends, but these days we tend to want to respond to every crisis. If we are humble enough to be willing to learn from those smaller faith communities who apply it more successfully, we can once again reclaim this essential aspect of the religious life.

A Ministry of Silence

I would like to close this contribution to the discussion on the future of Quaker involvement in interfaith sharing by making a few further suggestions which have arisen out of my own experience, and out of discussions with Friends who are involved in a personal way with beliefs and practices arising from other faith traditions. These are by no means the only way forward, and I am sure that there are other Friends who are contributing valuable ideas and service in this field. As I am no longer involved in the mainstream of Quaker work – and have not been for a number of years – I am not conversant with all the initiatives in which Friends are currently involved. But, with more than twenty years' involvement in Quaker interfaith work, I feel that I might make a few suggestions which can be discussed and worked upon, and which might enhance the distinctive Quaker work in this field.

The first suggestion must be that we do not lose sight of our heritage. If you have read so far, you will realise that Quakers have been involved in building bridges between spiritual traditions – not necessarily those of other faiths – since the 17th century. Our main contributions have been in sharing the depths of spiritual understanding, and, while facing and not fudging the differences, seeking points of understanding that come out of the deep silence where concepts and ideas fade away. If we can find harmony at this level, then we will also be able to share work on the concerns that will arise out of the open stillness, and with the shared ideas and intentions will come the power to see them through.

Many of the difficulties with interfaith work arise out of problems with language. In the stillness that is a gathered Quaker meeting – and this can also apply to a deeply shared group meditation – there are no problems with language. It is when we seek to describe the experience in words, and put it within the context of our own religious life, that we can have trouble. If we try to express these feelings without the experience of the shared silence, then it is even harder. So if Friends are going to make a contribution to interfaith theology, it should be a 'Theology of Silence'.

In their 1992 Swarthmore Lecture, *Images and Silence*, Chris Cook and Brenda Heales suggest that one of the most important things that Friends might do for the world is to offer a 'ministry of silence'. They suggest three ways in which this might be done, and all three have relevance for the future of Quaker interfaith work. (In the quotes which follow the emphasis is mine).

The first way of offering a ministry of silence would require Friends to do *what they have always done*, which is *to provide havens of silence for all, regardless of belief, orientation or race....*

The second way in which Friends might offer a ministry of silence is this: they might, *as individuals empowered by the silence of God consciously experienced*, offer a personal ministry of being a '*silence carrier'....*

The third way in which Friends might offer a ministry of silence *drawing upon the absolute silence of God* is by recognising a calling to a *ministry of being*.

All this requires Friends to practice this quality of silence in our meetings, and in our everyday lives. It also requires us to be willing to wait for a calling by the Spirit before such qualities are channelled into interfaith or any other kind of outward expression. I nearly said "*practical* expression", but this would be to miss the point that the achievement of deep word-less and thought-less silence is infinitely practical, regardless of whether we see the outward forms of it.

Other Ways forward

A final example of the differences in approach is in the area of interfaith prayer and worship. In 1983, the Committee for Relations with

People of Other Faiths of the British Council of Churches published a booklet called *Can We Pray Together? guidelines on worship in a multi-faith society.* Admittedly this was aimed at the mainstream churches, but it went to seemingly endless lengths to point out the problems (which I do not deny exist) of praying to or worshipping a God who is not in the Christian model. It is as if they went on the assumption that each religion prayed to a different God. While the booklet did keep the door open, and even gently encourage interfaith activities, the reservations were obvious.

At the same time as this booklet was being published, other groups such as The World Congress of Faiths had been holding interfaith services for many years, with a great deal of harmony and understanding. The Friends Interfaith Group was also facilitating groups based on the principle of mutual irradiation, which encouraged people to come together in a way that led to deep and lasting friendships across what might have been seen as 'barriers of faith', but were in fact found to be 'bridges of faith'. I was told that the BCC booklet had the effect of making some Christians, who had previously been happy with interfaith services to think again, but I do not think that it had any effect on the Quaker initiative. I am convinced that this is because silent sharing was the basis of our work, whereas others were slaves to words.

In a paper prepared for CIR in 1998 by Tom Gulliver, which arose out of discussions looking at a possible interfaith programme, he highlights four points which give an insight into "What is it to be a Quaker?". They are:

1. As Quakers we are committed to actualising That of God in everyone.
2. We have distinctive Quaker ways of pursuing that commitment through our discipline and testimonies, but we recognise that this commitment can be expressed in other ways.
3. Our understanding of God is experiential as we seek for spiritual truth in ourselves and others. We do not find it helpful to objectify God: indeed to do so can lead to distortion and misunderstanding.
4. God is present to us in our Meetings for Worship when the Spirit of Christ within each of us draws us together.

For me, this sums up very clearly the ideal Quaker approach to interfaith dialogue. If we truly seek to *actualise* That of God within all beings, then we *naturally* come to utilise the distinctive Quaker ways which have proved themselves over more than three centuries. As we seek to find God in our *experience,* and if we are firm in the knowledge that this truly *happens* in our worship, then we will want to base our dialogue on a spirit of worship. All faiths have their mystical elements, and we should seek to relate to them first, and then all the other things will be worked out in ways that we cannot imagine. Jesus told us that if we seek first the Kingdom of God, then everything else will be added. I have had the experience of seemingly insurmountable barriers breaking down when discussion follows a unifying silence, even though no effort was made to minimise the differences. I have found that following such silence there is a willingness to listen deeply, and to hear the spirit which underlies the words, rather than dwelling on the words themselves and immediately looking for difficulties. And this is not only my experience. It has been, in one way or another, that of Friends from the beginning.

If Quakers are to make any contribution to interfaith dialogue that has not already been made, we must follow our own testimony to the Power of the Spirit to work in silence to resolve all difficulties. We must, above all, be true to ourselves. As Lao Tzu says

[The Tao] (which has been equated with the Godhead)
... blunts edges
unties tangles
harmonises lights,
unites all dusts.[48]

This is another way of saying with George Fox that when "The Power of the Lord is over all" anything is possible. I believe that with this Power much can be accomplished, but without it there will only be a mess. With It, the world can be a better place; without It, things will only get worse.

Appendix 1

A collection of thoughts on interfaith understanding from Quaker and other sources; collected by Margot Tennyson.

THIS MATERIAL WAS originally published by the Friends Interfaith Group as Some Quaker Thoughts and Other Faiths *for the Interfaith Worship groups at Bradford Summer Gathering, 1992. It was later re-issued as a pamphlet by the Friends Interfaith Group, in the hope that Friends might also find it useful for Interfaith Services in which they might be involved, and for worship sharing, meditation and study groups in local meetings.*

I am sorry that no references were given in the pamphlet, and it has not been possible to trace the versions from which they come. Where specific books are known, acknowledgement has been given. I hope translators, authors and publishers will appreciate the spirit in which these are shared, and accept our acknowledgement and appreciation.

Be still and cool
In your own mind and spirit
From your own thoughts
And then you will feel the
Principle of God
> **George Fox,** *Quaker*
> (letter to Lady Claypole)

Be still and know that I Am God
> **Psalm 46,** *Jewish*

There is a light that shines beyond all things on earth, beyond us all, beyond the heavens, beyond the highest, the very highest heavens. This is the light that shines in our heart.

All this universe is in truth Brahman. He is the beginning and end of life and all. As such in silence, give him adoration.

There is a spirit that is mind and life, light and truth and vast spaces. He contains all works and desires and all perfumes and all tastes. He enfolds the whole universe, and in silence is loving to all.

This is the spirit that is in my heart, smaller than a grain of canary-seed, or the kernel of a grain of canary-seed. This is the spirit that is in my heart, greater than the earth, greater than the sky, greater than heaven itself, greater than the worlds.

He contains all works and desires and all perfumes and tastes. He enfolds the whole universe and in silence is loving to all. This is the spirit that is in my heart, this is Brahman.

Chandogya Upanishad, Hindu

I do my utmost to attain emptiness
I hold firmly to stillness.
The myriad creatures all return to their separate roots.
Returning to one's roots is known as stillness.
Tao Teh Ching, Taoist

The sign from God in Contemplation is silence, because it is impossible for a man to do two things at one time – he cannot both speak and meditate.

Through the faculty of meditation, man attains to eternal life; through it he receives the breath of the Holy Spirit – the bestowal of the Spirit is given in reflection and meditation.

Meditation is the key for opening the doors of the mysteries. In that state man abstracts himself; in that subjective mood he is immersed in the ocean of spiritual life and can unfold the secret of things-in-themselves.

Abdu'l-Baha, Baha'i

Be still
Expend not a breath in idle conversation
Put a seal on thy talk – God is the greatest.
Jami, Muslim

Lao Tzu says that "Silence is the great revelation". If we can penetrate this interior silence we will find a deep centre within which we can receive impressions from another plane. Like a calm pool reflects the moonbeam in the stillness of the night, equally, disturbing outer impressions will find a resting place, for in the silence everything is understood, in a way not comprehensible by the mind. Do not lead yourself to be analytical here for this is a divine process of transmutation where we can transcend the experience and offer it to the Beloved with a whole heart. A heart in the

state of becoming needs this inner well of silence, like the ego needs the
Higher Self, for only then can it drown in safety and be still.
Margaret Sampson, *Sufi*

☼ ☦ ☾ ✳ ☯ ✿ ॐ

There is a principle which is pure, placed in the human mind, which in
different places and ages has had different names; it is however pure and
proceeds from God. It is deep and inward, confined to no Forms of
Religion nor excluded from any, where the heart stands in perfect sincerity.
John Woolman, *Quaker;* Journals & Essays

There is a thing inherent and natural,
Which existed before heaven and earth.
Motionless and fathomless,
It stands alone and never changes;
It pervades everywhere and never becomes exhausted.
It may be regarded as the Mother of the Universe.
I do not know its name,
I am forced to give it a name,
I call it Tao, and I name it as supreme.
Tao Teh Ching, *Taoist*

Radiant is his light, yet invisible in the secret place of the heart, the Spirit
is the supreme abode wherein dwells all that moves and breathes and sees.
Know Him as all that is, and all that is not, the end of love-longing beyond
understanding, the highest of all beings.

He is self-luminous and more subtle than the smallest; but in Him rests
all the worlds and their beings. He is the everlasting Brahman, and He is
life and word and mind. He is truth and life immortal. He is the goal to
be aimed at: attain that goal.
Mundaka Upanishad, *Hindu*

Thy name is above all names, the most majestic and the most sublime.
The sound of Thy name is the sweetest the human ear can hear. Countless
persons call Thee simultaneously by Thy name and Thou dost hear them
all and respond to them. All at one and the same moment. Thou art the
same one God, but men give You many names.
Yasna, *Zoroastrian*

O God, whatever road I take joins the highway that leads to Thee.
Have the religions of mankind no common ground?
Is there not the same enrapturing beauty beaming forth from many
    hidden places?

101

Broad indeed is the carpet God has spread, and beautiful the colours
   He has given it ...
There is but one lamp in His house, in the rays of which,
Wherever I look, a bright assembly meets me.
O God, whatever road I take joins the highway that leads to Thee.
   Abulfazl, *Sufi*

The faiths of others all deserve to be honoured ...
by knowing them, one exalts one's own faith.
   Asoka, *Buddhist*

May the time be not distant, O God, when all your children will understand that they are brothers and sisters so that, one in spirit and one in
fellowship, they may be forever united before You. Then shall Your
Kingdom be established on earth, and the word of Your prophet shall be
fulfilled: "The Lord will reign for ever and ever".
   Prayer Book, *Jewish*

For, when I came into the silent assemblies of God's people, I felt a secret
power among them, which touched my heart; and as I gave way unto it I
found the evil weakening in me and the good raised up ...
   Robert Barclay, *Quaker*

Come, come whoever you are.
Worshipper, wanderer, lover of learning,
Ours is not a caravan of despair.
Even though you have broken your vows a thousand times
Come!
   Rumi, *Sufi*

God expects one thing of you, and that is that you should come out of
yourself in so far as you are a created being, and let God be God in you.
   Meister Eckhart, *Christian*

God, if I worship Thee in fear of hell
Burn me in hell.
If I worship Thee in hope of paradise
Exclude me from paradise.
But if I worship Thee for Thine own sake
Withhold not Thine Everlasting Beauty.
   Rabi'a, *Sufi*

102

There is, O monks, an Unborn, an Unmade, an Unmanifest and an Unbecome. If it were not so, there would be no escape from the born, the made, the manifest and the become.
> **The Buddha**

Jesus said:
When you make the two One
you will become Sons of Man,
and if you say,
"Mountain move away,"
it shall move.
> **Gospel of Thomas,** *Christian*

If your mind is open it is always ready for anything; it is open to everything. In the beginner's mind there are many possibilities; in the expert's mind there are few.
> **Shunryu Suzuki**; Zen Mind, Beginner's Mind

The Sage seeks Stillness in his heart,
and all things happen
as if by themselves.
> **The Tao Teh Ching,** *Taoist*

Let Peace fill your heart and mind and life. God never makes a mistake. If you do not understand, be patient and wait. In due time the Light will shine and you will understand.
> **White Eagle,** Heal Thyself

Our life is love, and peace, and tenderness and bearing one with another, and not laying accusations one against another; but praying one for another, and helping one another up with a tender hand.
> **Isaac Penington,** *Quaker – from his letters*

O God !
May I treat others
As I would be treated
What I like not for myself
May I dispense not to others.
> **Abdullah Ansari,** *Sufi*

Do not approve for another what you do not like for yourself.
> **Gospel of Zarathustra,** *Zoroastrian*

Do not do unto others that which you would not have them do unto you.
Rabbi Hillel, *Jewish*

Will ye tell others to be righteous and not practise righteousness yourself?
The Qur'an 2, 44

Since I joined the divine company of Holy men
All divisive tendencies of mind have vanished.
I have now neither an enemy nor an outsider
All I have befriended.
The doings of God I accept cheerfully,
This is the wise counsel received from the Guru.
Nanak rejoices at beholding God everywhere and in everyone.
Guru Granth Sahib, Love of Humanity, *Sikh*

Remembering that everywhere and in all people can be found some sort
of faith and righteousness. May we seek to foster this, and not destroy it.
May we not look for evil in one another, but for good.
Asoka, *Buddhist*

Show love to all creatures and thou wilt be happy, for when thou lovest
all things thou lovest the Lord, for He is in all.
Tulsi Das, *Hindu*

✡ ☧ ☾ ✴ ☯ ☸ ॐ

The Last Words of James Nayler

There is a spirit I feel delights to do no evil, nor to revenge any wrong,
but delights to endure all things, in hope to enjoy its own end. Its hope is
to outlive all wrath and contention, and to weary out all exaltation and
cruelty, or whatever is of a nature contrary to itself. It sees the end of all
temptations. As it bears no evil in itself, so it conceives none in thoughts
to any other. If it is betrayed, it bears it, for its ground and spring is in the
mercies and forgiveness of God. Its crown is meekness, its life is everlasting love unfeigned: it takes its kingdom with entreaty and not with
contention, and keeps it by lowliness of mind. In God alone can it rejoice,
though none else regard it, or can own its life. It's conceived in sorrow,
and brought forth without any pity to it, nor doth it murmur at grief and
oppression.
James Nayler, *Quaker*

Hatred is never diminished by hatred. Hatred is diminished by love. This
is the eternal law.
The Dhammapada, *Buddhist*

104

Return love for hatred.
Tao Teh Ching, *Taoist*

He alone will obtain an excellent end -
Who does good to others, and knows not how to reproach them,
Who is merciful to all creatures, and cherishes cattle;
And in the desert gives water to the thirsty:
Who is calm and never blames any.
Tukaram, *Hindu*

Be generous in prosperity, and thankful in adversity. Be worthy of the
trust of thy neighbour, and look upon him with a bright and friendly face.
He is a treasure to the poor, an admonisher to the rich, an answer to the
cry of the needy, a preserver of the sanctity of thy pledge. Be fair in thy
judgement, and guarded in thy speech. Be unjust to no man and show all
meekness to all men. Be as a lamp unto them that walk in darkness, a joy
to the sorrowful, a sea for the thirsty, a haven for the distressed, an upholder
and defender of the victim of oppression. Let integrity and uprightness
distinguish all thine acts.
Baha'U'llah, *Baha'i*

In the company of saints, man learns how to turn enemies into friends,
As he becomes completely free of evil, and bears malice to none,
In the company of the good, there is no swerving from the path,
No looking down upon anybody as evil.
Man sees all round him the Lord of Supreme Joy,
And freeing himself from the feverish sense of self,
Abandons all pride, such is the efficacy of fellowship with a holy man,
whose greatness is known only to the Lord.
The servant of the Ideal is akin to the Master.
Sukhmanu, *Sikh*

I forgive all living beings,
Let all living beings forgive me;
All in this world are my friends,
I have no enemies.
Prayer of Forgiveness, *Jain*

The humble, meek, merciful, just, pious and devout souls are everywhere
of one religion; and when death has taken off the masks, they will know
one another, though the diverse liveries they wear here make them
strangers.
William Penn, *Quaker*; Some Fruits of Solitude

Different creeds are but different paths to reach the Almighty. Various and different are the ways that lead to the temple of Mother Kali. Similarly various are the ways that lead to the house of the Lord. Every religion is nothing but one of these paths that lead to God.

Ramakrishna, *Hindu*

Even in error deem not the God of the Hindus to be other than the God of the Muslims, worship the one God, recognise the Enlightener. All men have the same human form. In all men blazes the same divine light. Love all God's creation, both the whole and every grain of sand. Love every leaf, every ray of light. Love the animals, love the plants, love each separate thing. If you love each thing then you will perceive the mystery of God in all, then you will thenceforth grow every day to a fuller understanding.

Feodor Dostoevsky, *Christian*, The Brothers Karamazov

O Thou who art the Kernel of Existence, reconcile us all into love of each other and of Thee, for all lamps are lit from the same Light.

Rumi, *Sufi*

O God, it is Thy word that mankind is a single nation, so all human beings are born free and equal in dignity and rights, they are endowed with love and conscience and should act towards one another in the spirit of brotherhood.

The Qur'an, *Islam*

Now is the time for the lover of God to raise high the banner of unity, to intone, in the assemblages of the world, the verses of friendship and love and to demonstrate to all that the grace of God is one. Thus will the tabernacles of holiness be upraised on the summits of the earth, gathering all peoples into the protective shadow of the World of Oneness. This great bounty will dawn over the world at the time when the lovers of God shall arise to carry out His teachings, and to scatter far and wide the fresh, sweet scent of universal love.

Baha'U'llah, *Baha'i*

Appendix 2

The Millennium Interfaith Invocation of Universal Love

THIS CELEBRATION WAS the last interfaith concern of Margot Tennyson. It was supported by Friends, other Christian groups, and by members of other faith communities. The Committee on Christian and Interfaith Relations minuted their support, and organisations such as The Interfaith Network, The World Congress of Faiths and the Westminster Foundation also wrote letters of goodwill which were quoted in the front of the special booklet which was published in advance of the event. In addition, representatives from the various faith communities who had known Margot and her work also wrote letters of support, and offered their help.

This was not only a celebration on one night. Margot's concern was that it should be an inspiration for various interfaith activities throughout the year 2000. Although, sadly, Margot was unable to be physically present at the celebration, we felt her presence with us, little knowing that she was about to pass on to the next stage of her life. She planned the programme for the evening, and expressed her vision in a letter, part of which was featured in the printed programme.

> My hope is that the joyfulness of this evening will stimulate many of you to prepare an interfaith event in your own area during the millennium. As I have been so immensely enriched in my spiritual journey by contact with people of different faiths, I feel confident in assuring you that you too will be enriched.

The atmosphere at the actual event, held at Friends House on the evening of Sunday 18th April 1999, was wonderfully peaceful and harmonious. Margot's Friend, Alec Davison, together with members of The Leaveners and volunteers from various London Meetings, organised the evening in an unobtrusively efficient way that ensured its smooth running, yet kept the spontaneous feeling that this was something that just happened. The participants, representing the Hindu, Jain, Buddhist,

107

Zoroastrian, Jewish, Christian, Muslim, Sikh and Baha'i communities, were supported by a mixed audience in which most of the faith communities were also represented.

There were dances from the Hindu Tagorean Society, and a short play on the life and enlightenment of the Buddha from a group of performers from the Chiswick Buddhist Vihara. Readings from the various scriptures were given by the Baha'i, Christian, Jewish, Muslim, and Zoroastrian participants, and we had some delightful singing from two Muslim children and from a choir from the Sikh Namdhari Education Group. Four members of the Quaker Youth Theatre acted out some of the writings of John Woolman which referred to his visit to the Native Americans. The theme of Universal Love permeated the whole performance, not only in the themes selected, but also in the feeling that was generated during the performance, and also afterwards, when all present were invited to join together for refreshments, which were provided without charge.

It is to be hoped that Margot's vision will be taken up, and that other groups, meetings and individual Friends will feel inspired to organise events on this theme throughout the millennium year. A specially prepared booklet, *Millennium Interfaith Invocation; Universal Love – a guide to help participants in an act of universal awareness*, written by Margot Tennyson and published by the Leaveners Press, is still (at the time of publication, 2000) available. It has many helpful aids including quotations, prayers, songs, chants, dances and a short play. There are also suggestions for school assemblies, the twinning of faith groups and an outline for an interfaith service. It is available from the Quaker Book Shop, Friends House, 173 Euston Road, London NW1 2BJ. Price £2.00 (p&p 50p).

The vision and the concern that produced the booklet and the event are best summed up by quoting from its back cover.

This guide has been produced by Margot Tennyson and friends from other faiths to enable others to participate in an act of interfaith activity of 'Universal Love' as part of the Millennium. It has been written in the belief that harmony between religions could be an important factor for world peace and co-operation, and it is offered as a modest contribution to the development of greater understanding and awareness of one another in the coming century.

Margot shares the view of Douglas Steere, who invites us to think of the great world religions as a row of summits in a common chain of mountains. If we do we might be able to counter the proverb, "*Mountains never meet*" with the observation that "*Men do meet*" and that when they do – on the deepest level – they confirm in each other the deepest thing each knows, and lift for each other a further curtain into ultimate truth.

Notes and References

Full publication details will be found in the bibliography

1. *The Journal and Major Essays of John Woolman*, edited by Phillips Moulton.
2. Bradford Smith, *Dear Gift of Life*.
3. [H.H. The] Dalai Lama, *Spiritual Advice for Buddhists and Christians*.
4. Frederick Parker-Rhodes, *The Friend*, vol. 135 (1977), p 636.
5. Marcus Braybrooke, *A Wider Vision: a History of the World Congress of Faiths*.
6. Ibid.
7. *The Journal of George Fox*, edited by John Nickalls.
8. I use the traditional Christian way of referring to God as 'Him' at this point because it is most relevant to the sense of what I am writing. I accept – as contemporary Quakers have discovered, partly due to the influence of other faiths – that there are times when it is just as acceptable, and maybe more accurate, to refer to God as 'She' or 'It'.
9. *King James' Bible*; Luke, 6:37.
10. Daisetz T Suzuki, *A Manual of Zen Buddhism*.
11. For more information on this subject see Marcus Borg, *Jesus and Buddha, the parallel sayings* and Roy Amore, *Two Masters, One Message*; details in bibliography.
12. *The Journal of George Fox*, edited by John Nickalls.
13. William Penn; Preface to *The Journal of George Fox*.
14. *The Journal of George Fox*, edited by John Nickalls.
15. N. I. Matar, Some Notes on George Fox and Islam; *Journal of the Friends Historical Society*, Volume 55, No. 8, FHS 1989.
16. Quoted in Margot Tennyson, *Friends and Other Faiths*.
17. For detailed information about the divisions among Friends in the USA, see H. Larry Ingle, *Quakers in Conflict; The Hicksite Reformation*, University of Tennessee Press, 1986.
18. 'M' (Mahendranath Gupta), *Gospel of Sri Ramakrishna*, (Abridged Edition) page 460.
19. Information about the Fellowship of Friends of Truth has been taken from contemporary minutes and some private papers passed to the author.

20. Douglas Steere; *Mutual Irradiation*.
21. Translation by a Turkish Sufi friend of the author.
22. *The Seeker*, Spring 1999.
23. Information about the Open Letter Movement is summarised from correspondence with a member of their 'Nucleus'.
24. John Linton, *Quakerism as Forerunner*.
25. *The Universalist*; October 1998.
26. Damaris Parker-Rhodes, *Truth, a Path and not a Possession*.
27. Frederick Parker-Rhodes' spiritual philosophy and mystical insight is succinctly summed up in *Wholesight*, Pendle Hill Pamphlet #217.
28. Founding statement of the Friends Interfaith Group largely composed by Margot Tennyson.
29. John Edward Southall, *The Power of Stillness*, 1900. Edited version published by Quaker Home Service as a leaflet entitled *Silence*.
30. *Quaker Faith and Practice*; 19.21.
31. Ibid; 19.08.
32. Ibid; 2.02
33. Definition given in a talk on meditation given in London in the early 1970s by Swami Chidananda, Head of the Divine Life Society, India.
34. *Isa Upanishad*, vs. 5, 6, translated by Patrick Olivelle.
35. *Tao Teh Ching, The Way of the Ways*, translated by Herrymon Maurer.
36. *King James' Bible*; John, 1:1 – 3.
37. Swami Tripurananda in *Three Spiritual Journeys*.
38. Marjorie Sykes, *Transcending Tradition*.
39. Martha Dart, *Marjorie Sykes, Quaker Gandhian*.
40. Quoted in Marjorie Sykes, *Transcending Tradition*.
41. Also quoted in Marjorie Sykes, *Transcending Tradition*.
42. M.M. Gidvani: *Shah Abdul Latif*, The India Society, London, 1922.
43. The story of Hayy ibn Yaczan (Hai bin Yaqzan) and the involvement with Quakers is taken from an unpublished manuscript, *Journey Into the Orient* by Jeanette Bossert, which was given to me by the author for use in interfaith work. I hope that it will be published one day.
44. Ibid.
45. Ibid. The story is also told in *The Journey of the Soul* by Abu Bakr Muhammed bin Tufail, translated by Dr Riad Kocache, Octagon Press, London, 1982.
46. Maha Ghosananda; *Step by Step*.
47. The three papers were: *A Place in the Dialogue* by Hugh Pyper; *One Truth, Many Religions* by Rex Ambler; and *Of Faiths and Cultures* by Eleanor Nesbitt.
48. *Tao Teh Ching, The Way of the Ways*, translated by Herrymon Maurer.

Bibliography

This bibliography consists of books mentioned in the text, other titles that relate to the text (though not specifically mentioned), and a few titles that have been helpful to the author in preparing this book, and in his understanding of other faith traditions. (o/p indicates that the publication is out of print)

Alexander, Horace; *The Meeting Place of the World's Great Faiths*, Quaker Universalist Pamphlet #2. Quaker Universalist Group. (QUG) London.

Amore, Roy C; *Two Masters, One Message, the lives and teachings of Gautama and Jesus*, Abingdon Press, Nashville, 1978.

Arriens, Jan; *The Place of Jesus in Quaker Universalism*, Quaker Universalist Pamphlet #17. (QUG)

Bancroft, Anne; Newman, Rabbi Jeffrey; Tripurananda, Swami; *Three Spiritual Journeys*, Friends Interfaith Group, 1984. (o/p)

Bills, David; *The Ripening of Quaker Worship*; the 27th Annual Quaker Lecture in Florida, South-eastern Y.M., Florida, 1997.

Borg, Marcus; (ed) *Jesus and Buddha – the parallel sayings*, Ulysses Press, Berkeley, California, 1997.

Braybrooke, Marcus; *A Wider Vision, a History of the World Congress of Faiths*, OneWorld, Oxford, 1996.

Britain Yearly Meeting; *Advices and Queries*, BYM 1995.

Britain Yearly Meeting; *Quaker Faith and Practice*, BYM 1994.

Cohen, J M and Phipps, J-F; *The Common Experience*, Rider Books 1979. (o/p)

Committee for Relations with People of Other Faiths, British Council of Churches; *Can We Pray Together?*, BCC 1983. (o/p)

Cook, Chris and Heales, Brenda; *Images and Silence*, (the 1992 Swarthmore Lecture), QHS 1992.

Crom, Scott; *Quaker Worship and Techniques of Meditation*; Pendle Hill Pamphlet #195, 1974. (o/p)

[H.H. The] Dalai Lama; *The Good Heart; A Buddhist Perspective on the Teachings of Jesus*, Rider Books, 1997.

[H.H. The] Dalai Lama; *Spiritual Advice for Christians and Buddhists*, edited by Donald W. Mitchell; Continuum Books, New York, 1998.

Dart, Martha; *To Meet at The Source: Hindus and Quakers*, Pendle Hill Pamphlet #289.

Dart, Martha; *Marjorie Sykes, Quaker Gandhian*, Sessions Book Trust, 1993.

Dinshaw, Nadir (compiler) *A Wide Open Heart: An Interfaith Anthology of Christian Comment*, available from Friends Book Centre, London.

Fox, George; *Journal*, edited by John L Nickalls, Religious Society of Friends, London, 1975.

Fozdar, Jamshed; *The God of Buddha*, Asia Publishing, New York, 1973. (o/p)

Franck, Frederick; *A Little Compendium on That Which Matters*, St Martin's Press, New York, 1993. (o/p)

Gabb, W.J; *The Goose is Out*, The Buddhist Society 1956. (o/p)

Gillman, Harvey; *A Minority of One, a journey with Friends*, (the 1988 Swarthmore Lecture) QHS 1988.

Goldsmith, Joel S.; *The Contemplative Life: a new text for personal growth and extended awareness*, L. N. Fowler, 1963.

Gorman, George; *The Amazing Fact of Quaker Worship* (The 1973 Swarthmore Lecture), QHS 1988.

Graham, Dom Aelred; *Conversations Christian and Buddhist*, Collins, 1969. (o/p)

Irie, Yukio; *Pilgrimage Towards the Fountainhead: Quakerism and Zen Buddhism Today*. The tenth James Backhouse Lecture, Australia Yearly Meeting, 1973. (o/p)

Irie, Yukio; *A Zen-Christian Pilgrimage: The fruits of ten annual colloquia in Japan 1967-1976*; The Zen-Christian Colloquium 1981. (o/p)

Lacout, Pierre; *God is Silence*, pocket edition, QHS 1993.

Lawrence, Brother; *Practice of the Presence of God*, Samata Books, Madras, 1987 (also published by several UK publishers).

Linton, John; *Quakerism as Forerunner*, Quaker Universalist Group pamphlet #1.

'M' (Mahendranath Gupta); *Gospel of Sri Ramakrishna*, (abridged edition), translated into English with an introduction by Swami Nikhilananda, Ramakrishna Vedanta Center, New York, 1974.

[Ven.] Maha Ghosananda; *Step by Step – meditations on wisdom and compassion*, Parallax Press, Berkeley, California, 1992.

Maw, Geoffrey; *Pilgrims in Hindu Holy Land*, ed. Gillian M (Maw) Conacher and Marjorie Sykes, Sessions, York, 1997.

Mitchell, Stephen; *The Gospel of Jesus*, Rider, 1991.

Murphy, Carol; *The Sound of Silence – moving with T'ai Chi*; Pendle Hill Pamphlet #205, 1976.

Newman, Rabbi Jeffrey; see Bancroft, Anne, *Three Spiritual Journeys*.

Parker-Rhodes, Damaris; *Truth, A Path not a Possession*, (Swarthmore `Lecture 1977), QHS 1977.

Parker-Rhodes, Damaris; *The Way Out is the Way In*, QHS, 1985.

Pym, Jim; *Listening to the Light; how to bring Quaker simplicity and integrity into our lives*; Rider Books, London, 1999.

Pym, Jim; *What Kind of God, What Kind of Healing?*, Friends Fellowship of Healing, 1990. Revised edition published by The Spiritual Healing Society, 1999.

Ramana Maharshi; *The Teachings of Ramana Maharshi*, edited by Arthur Osborne, Rider, London, 1962.

Ross, Hugh McGregor; *Jesus Untouched by the Church, His Teachings in the Gospel of Thomas*, calligraphy by John Blamires, (includes a translation of the Gospel) Sessions of York 1998.

Smith, Bradford; *Dear Gift of Life, a man's encounter with death*; Pendle Hill Pamphlet # 142.

Smith, Bradford; *Meditation the Inward Art*; George Allen and Unwin, London, 1964. (o/p)

Sox, David; *John Woolman, 1720-1772, Quintessential Quaker*, Sessions of York, and Friends United Press, Indiana, 1999.

Steere, Douglas V; *Mutual Irradiation*, Pendle Hill Pamphlet #175.

Sykes, Marjorie; *An Indian Tapestry, Quaker threads in the history of India, Pakistan and Bangladesh from the seventeenth century to independence*; (a revised and updated version of *Quakers in India*). Compiled and edited by Geoffrey Carnall, with a final chapter by him taken from notes by Marjorie Sykes, Sessions of York, 1997.

Sykes, Marjorie; *Quakers in India*, George Allen and Unwin, London 1980. (o/p)

Sykes, Marjorie; *Transcending Tradition: excerpts from the writings and talks of Marjorie Sykes*, compiled and edited by Martha Dart, Sessions, York, 1995.

Tamura, Teruyasu; *A Zen Buddhist Encounters Quakerism*, Pendle Hill Pamphlet #302.

Tennyson, Margot; *Friends and Other Faiths*, Quaker Home Service, 1992.

Tennyson, Margot; *The Inner and the Outer Become One*, published by the author, London 1992. (o/p)

Tripurananda, Swami; see Bancroft, Anne, *Three Spiritual Journeys*.

Walker, Susan, (ed); *Speaking of Silence; Christians and Buddhists on the Contemplative Way*; Paulist Press, 1987. (o/p)

Wilson, Paul; *The Little Book of Calm*, Penguin Books 1998.

Woolman, John; *Journal and Major Essays* edited by Phillips Moulton, Oxford University Press, New York, 1971. Reprinted by Friends United Press, Richmond Indiana.

Journals and magazines

The Friend, independent Quaker weekly, New Premier House, 150 Southampton Road, London WC1.

Journal of the Friends Historical Society, c/o Friends House Library.

The Middle Way; journal of The Buddhist Society, 53 Eccleston Square, London SW1.

The Seeker; journal of the Seekers' Association.

The Universalist; journal of the Quaker Universalist Group.

Vedanta East and West; journal of the Ramakrishna Vedanta Centre, Blind Lane, Bourne End, Bucks.

Quaker Monthly, Quaker Home Service, Friends House.

Translations – scriptures and other source books

There are many translations available of most of the world's scriptures and religious writings. I have only listed those that I have quoted from, or those which have been of particular help to me, and in the editions that I have available. Details of other versions can be obtained from The Quaker Bookshop, Friends House, Euston Road, London NW1 2BJ or from any good bookshop. I am sure that readers will discover – or even already have – their own favourites. Titles marked * are also available – though in different translations – in Penguin editions, which may be more easily accessible.

**The Bhagavad Gita*; translated by Swami Nikhilananda, Ramakrishna-Vivekananda Center, New York, 1974.

The Bible; Authorised [King James'] Version. (Many publishers)

*The Dhammapada; translated by Rev. Jack Austin, The Buddhist Society, London 1988.

The Essential Rumi; translated by Colemen Barks with John Moyne, Castle Books, 1997.

The Lotus Sutra; translated by Burton Watson.

**The Qur'an*; translated by M. H Shakir, Tahrike Tarsile Qur'an Inc., New York, 1997.

A Manual of Zen Buddhism; D.T. Suzuki, with translations and commentary by the author. Published for the Buddhist Society, London, by Rider and Co., 1957.

**Tao Teh Ching; The Way of the Ways*; translated by Herrymon Maurer, Fellowship in Prayer, New Jersey, 1982, and Wildwood House, London 1989.

Teachings of the Buddha; new edition of 'The Gospel of Buddha' compiled and translated by Paul Carus, and edited and revised by Diana St Ruth, Rider Books, 1998.

*The Upanishads; a new translation by Patrick Olivelle, Oxford World's Classics 1996.

**Zen Flesh, Zen Bones*; Zen stories and teachings translated by Paul Reps and Nyogen Senzaki, Charles Tuttle 1957.

Resources and Useful Addresses

Quaker groups

(The following can all be contacted via Friends House, Euston Road, London NW1 2BJ. (Tel. 020 7663 1000). Most of the special interest groups connected with Friends are run by volunteers, and the names of the secretaries and other officers change from time to time. The names and addresses of the contact people can be found in the current Book of Meetings.*)*

Quaker Committee for Christian and Inter-faith Relationships.
The Quaker Universalists.
The Seekers.
The Open Letter Movement.
Quaker Green Concern.
Friends Fellowship of Healing.
(For further details of these Quaker special interest groups, see the text, or the current *Book of Meetings* (obtainable from the Quaker Bookshop).

The Quaker Bookshop, stocks many books on other faiths, meditation etc., and most Quaker publications from other Yearly Meetings. Anything not in stock can be ordered. It is also situated at Friends House. Their direct telephone number is 020 7663 1031. Details of any other Quaker publications mentioned in the text, and not listed separately, can be obtained from the Library at Friends House.

Woodbrooke Quaker Study Centre
1046 Bristol Road, Selly Oak,
Birmingham B29 6LJ
Tel. 0121-472 5171
Woodbrooke runs an increasing number of courses relating to interfaith matters.

Charney Manor
Charney Bassett, Wantage,
Oxfordshire OX12 0EJ
Tel. 01235 868206
Charney Manor is a Quaker retreat and conference centre. They have a number of courses relating to Quakers and other faiths.

Other Useful Addresses

The World Congress of Faiths
2 Market Street, Oxford OX1 3EF
Tel. 01865 202751.

Two other similar organisations also share offices with the WCF. They are the International Interfaith Centre (Tel 01865 202745) and the International Association for Religious Freedom (Tel. 01865 202744).

The Interfaith Network
5-7 Tavistock Place, London WC1 9SS
Tel. 020 7388 0008.

WCF and IFN are probably the principal bodies for information about the various faith communities currently functioning in Britain today. They have on their councils representatives of most of the major faith groups, and are willing and able to provide contact addresses either by post (SAE please) or telephone.

The Festival Shop
56 Poplar Road, Kings Heath, Birmingham B14 7AG
Tel 0121 444 0444

The Festival Shop is a centre for multifaith and multicultural resources. They publish and distribute a range of multifaith calendars, books, cards, posters and other resources for all ages. They supply by post, and issue a colourful and interesting catalogue.

Greensleeves Books
2 Market Street, Chipping Norton, Oxfordshire OX7 5NQ

Greensleeves Books are specialists in books on mysticism and comparative religion, new and second-hand. They have a book-finding service for out-of-print titles.

Contacts in the USA

Pendle Hill Quaker Study Centre (also Pendle Hill Publications)
Plush Mill Road, Wallingford, Pa. 19086 USA

Pendle Hill is a Quaker study centre in Philadelphia which has a number of courses relating to various themes considered in this book. They also publish the excellent Pendle Hill Pamphlet series, and a number of books.

Quaker Universalist Fellowship
c/o Sally Rickerman
121 Watson Mill Road, Landenberg, Philadelphia 19350-9344 USA
(QUF publish a number of booklets on interfaith themes, as well as a magazine)

Fellowship in Prayer
291 Witherspoon Street, Princeton, New Jersey 08542 USA.
(Publishers of the excellent magazine, *Sacred Journey*)